*Novitiate*

CISTERCIAN STUDIES SERIES: NUMBER TWENTY-FIVE

HOLY CROSS ABBEY
NOVITIATE

# CHRIST THE WAY

CISTERCIAN STUDIES SERIES: NUMBER TWENTY-FIVE

# Christ the Way

*The Christology of Guerric of Igny*

John Morson ocso

CISTERCIAN PUBLICATIONS
Kalamazoo, Michigan
1978

Cistercian Studies Series ISBN 0-87907-800-6

This Volume ISBN 0-87907-825-1

Cistercian Publications, Inc.
1749 W. Michigan—WMU
Kalamazoo, MI 49008

*Library of Congress Catalog Card Number:* 74-8591

© COPYRIGHT, John Morson, 1972

Available in Europe and the Commonwealth from A.R. Mowbray & Co. Ltd., St Thomas House, Becket Street, Oxford OX1 15J.

# CONTENTS

# INTRODUCTION

O N AUGUST 19TH the Cistercian Order keeps the
feast of Blessed Guerric. It was on this day, in the year
1157, that this second Abbot of Igny died, almost
exactly three years after his master, Saint Bernard of Clairvaux.

We may learn something about him from the *Exordium
Magnum*, the 'Great Early History' of the Order.[1] It is so
called to distinguish it from the *Parvum Exordium,* a work
much smaller, but of greater historical value. The *Exordium
Magnum* is a highly imaginative account of the Cistercian
Order's early saints, composed a century or more after the
foundation of Citeaux. In the two chapters devoted to
Guerric of Igny[2] we read that he died "full of days." If that
could mean ninety for us now, it may have meant no more
than seventy when medicine was in such a primitive state and
the expectation of life so much shorter. The age of seventy
would place Guerric's birth between 1085 and 1090, but he
may have been born earlier; in any case, just at the time when
Hildebrand's reforms and centralized government were giving
the Church some of the freedom from secular control and the
renewed-vitality which it so badly needed.

The age into which Guerric was born, however different
from our own, still had some likenesses. There were not only
canon lawyers; there were also pioneers in speculative theolo-

1. *Exordium Magnum Cisterciense,* ed. Bruno Griesser, Rome (Editiones Cistercienses), 1961. Not yet in English.
2. Distinction 3, chapters 8 and 9.

gy. Men like Saint Peter Damian had come and gone, leaving
the Church richer for their passing. There were still spiritual
leaders of the kind which the late twentieth century likes to
call "charismatic." Robert of Molesme was near the end of a
long life, in which he had patiently undertaken one monastic
reform after another. Guerric may have been hardly more
than a boy at the Cathedral school of Tournai (now in the
middle of Belgium) at the time of Robert's last enterprise,
the foundation of a monastery in flat marshy country near
Dijon, which received the name of *Cistercium*: Cîteaux. Little
was known of this monastery for about fifteen years. Then a
party of young noblemen shocked their friends and relatives
(in one or two cases even their wives) by deciding that this
life of withdrawal from the world, austerity and prayer in
common, was to be theirs.

Of course these men who went to Cîteaux were strongly
influenced by a leader. This was Bernard of Fontaines, gifted
and handsome, born to influence and lead others wherever he
went, without necessarily having any clear intention or desire
to lead. Cîteaux began to make foundations. One of the earliest, and soon the most prolific, had Bernard as its abbot. He
commited all the imprudences which one expects in a man
who leads others simply by the force of his genius and personality, and was himself soon incapable of living the common monastic life. But when ten years had passed Clairvaux
was one of the best known monasteries in Europe. From
being simply abbot of Clairvaux Bernard became a force to
be reckoned with in the secular as well as in the ecclesiastical
world.

Up in the north Guerric had spent the first part of his life
in academic circles, but he too was touched by the movement
of monastic reform and by the enthusiasm for return to first
souces. Like the Cistercians, he was traditional but in a different way. He retired into a hermitage near Tournai's Cathedral Church. Even so, he could not fail to hear about the
abbot of Clairvaux. It is a tribute to Bernard's reputation for
purely spiritual wisdom — apart from political genius — that
Guerric was enticed from his solititude. He went to talk to

Bernard in his monastery, perhaps as someone seeking God in
our time might have gone to a Padre Pio at San Giovanni
Rotondo, without the intention of following an entirely new
vocation. But Clairvaux became his home for about the next
thirteen years. By that time a new abbot was needed in one
of Clairvaux's daughter houses. The hermit of Tournai became the abbot of Igny.

This monastery was evidently flourishing, but we know few
details of its history in the period, nearly twenty years, which
passed until Guerric's death. What we know about Guerric
himself is simply the self-revelation found in his fifty-four
sermons, composed for the seasons and feasts of the Church's
year. Even if they need some translation, not only into words
but also into concepts of our contemporaries, they still express with clarity and elegance themes which are basic to the
Christian spirituality of any century.[3]

If it were not so, there would hardly have been a demand
for a new edition and then for a translation into English. The
critical edition has been based on nine manuscripts which
come from the two centuries after the author's death.[4] The
English translation has been made from this text, the nearest
possible, it would seem, to what Guerric himself wrote.[5] The
work of editing has been supplemented by the further study
which is now being introduced.

In 1935 Dom Déodat De Wilde, now abbot of the Cistercian
Abbey near Westmalle, Belgium, published his *De Beato
Guerrico abbate Igniacensi eiusque doctrina de formatione
Christi in nobis.*[6] *Forma* is a key-word for Guerric, and *for-*

3. The historical study of Guerric has been undertaken at greater length, with
indication of sources and authorities, in the Introductions to the critical edition
and to the English translation. See notes 4 and 5.

4. *Guerric d'Igny, Sermons.* Series *Sources chrétiennes,* nn. 166, 202, Cerf,
Paris, 1970, 1973. Introduction, critical text and notes, by John Morson and
Hilary Costello. French translation under the direction of Placide Deseille.

5. Guerric of Igny, *Liturgical Sermons,* 2 vols; Cistercian Fathers Series, nn. 8
and 32; Spencer, Massachusetts, 1970, 1971. Introduction and translation by
monks of Mount Saint Bernard Abbey.

6. In the nineteen-thirties any theological thesis for a Roman University had to
be presented in Latin. De Wilde's work has never been published in a vernacular
language.

*matio* expresses for him the causality by which we are made
to share in the divine life of Christ. It leads straight into the
part played by Mary in our sanctification. Whatever the nature of Christ's action in us, his *forming* his own likeness,
Mary is at work under Christ himself, drawing all her efficacy
from him.

After De Wilde's masterly exposition, it seemed clear that,
if a second study of Guerric was to be published, it would
have to follow a different line.

The sermons are concerned with the Mysteries of God
made Man. The Incarnation — the attainment of its purpose
in our Redemption and Sanctification: everything comes
under this. Christ the Way — the Way because he is the Truth
and the Life: here we found the theme on which we should
have to reflect, discerning just what Guerric had taken from
the greatest of the Fathers before him, how he had synthe-
sized, what he had contributed himself to that work of hand-
ling on which makes Christian tradition.

Of the three parts which make up this book, the first is
concerned principally with giving Guerric of Igny his place in
the historical development of the Church's teaching concerning the central Mystery of Christ the Son of God. It deals
with his sources, but especially his use of the Bible and the
advantages, and also the difficulties, attaching to a presenta-
tion of Guerric in the late twentieth century. The second
chapter treats of the assumption of our human nature as
Christ's greatest humiliation, but also his supreme triumph; his
Virgin Mother necessarily finds her place here. Some account
has been given of the types and allegories chosen by the
author from the inspired books and from the Fathers who
have written before him. Since this study is meant not simply
for antiquarians, an attempt has been made to put Guerric
into relation with modern and contemporary theologians;
even to enquire whether he has something to contribute to
the difficult question of the knowledge and bliss possessed by
Christ during his life on earth. The third chapter looks to the
purpose of that condescension on God's part: Mediation and
Redemption. It is impossible, when dealing with a writer like

Guerric to separate these from our individual sanctification, our progress in union with God, to be consummated by the face-to face vision of his glory.

### ACKNOWLEDGMENTS

The first acknowledgement must be to Father Hilary Costello of Mount Saint Bernard Abbey, who has shared with me the labor of producing the critical edition of Guerric's sermons, on which this study is based. The pages which follow would have been more disorderly, the style more crude, if it had not been for the stimulus and wise advice given by Father Gervais Dumeige of the Gregorian University, Rome, and by Dom Jean Leclercq of Clervaux, Luxemburg. The study of Guerric could not have been undertaken but for my religious superiors, who have allowed me to give my time to this. The initiative was taken by the late Abbot General, Dom Gabriel Sortais, an outstanding patron of monastic studies, who enabled the series *Textes monastiques d'Occident* to find its place within the well known *Sources chrétiennes*. Dom Gabriel invited me to collaborate with Father Placide Deseille in the work of editing; thus in the course of time came the critical edition of Guerric and the small study presented here. An earlier recension, substantially the same as what follows, has appeared already in the pages of *Cîteaux*, volume 22 (1971). I am grateful to the editor for allowing me to retain the copyright.

# PART ONE

"Turn Your Ear, and Listen to the Word of the Wise."

CHAPTER ONE

# GUERRIC'S PLACE IN TRADITION

G UERRIC OF IGNY comes at the end of a long tradition of patristic theology. If this patristic theology is
distinguished from what came afterwards, in fact scholastic, this is not done with an a priori bias, as though the
Fathers had almost a monopoly on something which the
scholastics lost. But it is impossible to dispute that there is a
tradition of a meditative theology based immediately upon
scriptural texts, and that this tradition finds its place between
two tendencies which are largely occupied with elaborating
and clarifying concepts.

I have deliberately spoken of two *tendencies,* not of two
*periods,* because the development and the succession are
chronological only in a very vague sense. Not only do the
tendencies overlap, but in the most gifted of the Fathers or
of the Scholastics the two are found side by side. One thinks
of the school of Saint Victor, but most especially of Saint
Anselm. He finds dialectic and warmth of devotion entirely
compatible, as in his *Why was God made Man? (Cur Deus
homo?* He is praying to God but a line of argument finds its
way in.

A "conceptual" theology is one which, because it is discur-
sive and follows every statement to a logical conclusion,
rightly insists upon a precise and correct definition of terms
and ideas. At the present time this word "conceptual" is
often used in a belittling sense. It is not so in these pages, for
the writings of different men, even different writings of one

3

and the same man, have had to assume such or such a character by force of circumstances. We read Saint Clement of
Rome, Saint Ignatius of Antioch, the Shepherd of Hermas or
the Epistle of Barnabas, and we do not think of them as
conceptual. It is otherwise when we come to Origen, above
all to his *First Beginnings (Peri archôn)*. The Alexandrines
insisted upon speculation, upon precise definition of terms
and classification of categories. Origen, like Clement his
predecessor, had to watch over the "new theology," even to
baptize it. Here was a fore-runner of scholasticism indeed. His
reputation with Fathers after him was rather perplexing, e.g.
with Saint Jerome, who condemned Origen while he was
using him. Did Jerome perhaps oppose Origen because Rufinus admired him? The strongest condemnation came from
the fifth ecumenical Council.[1] But that Council was a very
political affair, and the almost global condemnation may not
have been directed against Origen himself so much as might
first appear. However that may be, we are in a better position
than the Fathers of the early centuries to ponder the question: what would have happened to theology, even to the
simple Christian faith, if Origen had not been there? Would
there have been a Cyril of Alexandria, would there have been
even a Council of Ephesus? Certainly these may seem idle
questions, and it is not enough to ask them. To answer any
one of them could be the work of an entire book. They are
suggested here as a matter for reflection, only because if we
are to understand and to appreciate an author who wrote
centuries later, we must know where to place him; and to do
this we must recognize some main outlines and some different tendencies in tradition, above all we must see the com-
plexities which bore, directly or indirectly, upon the author
whom we are studying. Besides Origen's polemical and more
highly systematized works — some would say his strictly
theological works, though this may be begging a question —
there are his homilies and commentaries on the Bible. The
two approaches can be found not only in the one man, but
even in one of his works, notably in the commentary on

1. DS 433: cf 403-411.

Saint John's Gospel.[2] Furthermore, there are commentaries on books of the Bible which have provided unadulterated nourishment for monks in their cloisters through the centuries and were read in the monastic liturgy. Now after the second Vatican Council they can be read in the liturgy again. The author of *First Principles* and *Against Celsus* has also given us such commentaries or homilies as those on the Book of Numbers.[3] The enumeration of the stopping places in the journey of the Israelites through the desert of Sinai is not very promising material. But it prompted Origen to produce a text which has become classical in spiritual literature: his description of the stages in our spiritual journey. Saint Bernard is best known for the sermons which form his commentary on the Song of Songs.[4] William of Saint Thierry was writing such a commentary at about the same time.[5] Bernard left his work unfinished; after his death it was continued in fear and trembling by Gilbert of Hoyland[6] and was finally brought to completion by another English Cistercian, John of Ford.[7] When mediaevalists study the commentaries on the *Song of Songs* they have to keep in mind that this tradition goes back to Saint Hippolytus of Rome and to Origen of Alexandria.[8] Others were not slow to follow: Saint Gregory of Nyssa in the East; Saint Gregory the Great in the West (though we have only an inaccurate account of the sermons which he preached);[9] in later centuries Rupert of Deutz. The twelfth century was to see the efflorescence.

---

2. E.g. Origen's Commentary on Saint John's Gospel contains an early elucidation of the trinitarian dogma: Ed. E. Preuschen, GCS 10:33,39.

3. Origen, *Homelies sur les Nombres,* SCh 29 (1959).

4. OB 1 and 2.

5. *Exposition on the Song of Songs,* SCh 82 (1962); CF 6 (1970).

6. PL 184:11-252.

7. The sermons of John of Ford have recently been published from the single extant manuscript in CCL Cont Med 17. The editors are Edmund Mikkers and Hilary Costello, who has been my collaborator in editing the fifty-four sermons of Guerric. The English translation for the Cistercian Fathers Series is in preparation.

8. For Saint Hippolytus see G. Bardy, SCh 14: 28-54. For the relationship between Origen and Hippolytus see O. Rousseau, SCh 37: 13-17.

9. For Saint Gregory the Great see P. Verbraken, Introduction to CCL 144, with citation from a letter of Gregory.

So, from the second and third centuries, two trends in Christian thought are easily discernible; the two ways of reflecting upon the truth revealed by God through Jesus Christ, in fact two kinds of theology. Some will say at once that this is an over-simplification. It is true that not everthing which has ever been written can be put at once into one of these two categories; but the distinction is valid up to a point, and can legitimately serve a purpose in this opening chapter. The one is speculative, elaborating, conceptual; usually it has to be such, for its origin is polemical, or at least it is being applied as a corrective to something which would otherwise be an aberration. The second way might be difficult and even dangerous without the first. It is, under the influence of the Holy Spirit, a prayerful reflection upon God's revealed word and all the depths of meaning which it contains, with complete detachment from, perhaps ignorance of, any politics or controversies. If we may borrow an idea from centuries after Origen — this theology prefers to feel or to experience compunction, desire and love, rather than to give a scientific definition of any of these. So of course does every true Christian. The first way is that of intellectual analysis, the second underlines heavily the value of experience: "Love itself is knowledge." Some will say that the first way conforms better to our idea of the scientific. Some will say that the first is theology and the second is not; then others will answer that such a restricted idea of theology is arbitrary, and that any seriously applied reflection upon God and what he has revealed deserves this name. Certainly for the Greeks, and for other Eastern Christians, the real *theologos* was the one who passed from sorrow *(penthos)* and action *(praxis)* to contemplation *(theôria)*, the one who was willing and able to forget all else, to remove every obstruction to the movement of the Spirit and to let God penetrate him with a sense of his presence. He was a man who spoke to God, to whom God spoke in turn, who could speak of God to others. It was only later, and especially in the West, that the word became reserved for those who used a more highly developed technique of thought and expression when they discussed or defended God's revealed truth.

I have dwelt upon Origen because, even with the morsel of his writings which has been preserved, it seems evident that two main trends of Christian thought, we may even say two kinds of theology, are strikingly exemplified in this one man. This is not to say that he stands entirely alone. There is Saint Gregory of Nyssa. If we read his commentary on the Song of Songs,[10] then the same teaching summed up in his *Life of Moses*,[11] we must conclude that there are very few Fathers of the Church who have made such an original and such a rich contribution to our spiritual tradition. All that is best in Denys the Areopagite is found already in Gregory of Nyssa. But then we can remember that Gregory had also to write the *Adversus Eunomium*,[12] had to carry on controversy against Tritheists, Apollinarists and *Pneumatomachoi*. In both senses he was continuing the work undertaken by his brother, Saint Basil the Great. Basil's work *De Spiritu Sancto*,[13] taken alone, is certainly controversial, but it has entitled him to be regarded as one of the founders of Eastern spirituality. With his Rules[14] he became for the monastic East at least as important as Saint Benedict was to be for the West.

Above all there is Saint Augustine of Hippo. The history of the Church has hardly recorded such a controversial writer. He had to devote much of his life to refuting four heresies: the Manichaeans, the Pelagians, some die-hards in Gaul who, more than a thousand years later would be rather unkindly nick-named the Semi-Pelagians, and finally the Donatists. But at the same time Saint Augustine is a founder of Western spirituality and mysticism. Those extensive controversial writings come from the same pen as the sermons to the people, the *Discourses on the Psalms*,[15] the *Commentary on Saint John's*

10. PG 44:755-1120.

11. PG 44:297-430.

12. PG 45:243-1122.

13. PG 32:67-218; tr. B. Jackson in *The Select Library of Nicene and Post-Nicene Fathers of the Christian Church*, 2nd Series, vol. 8 (Grand Rapids: Eerdmans, 1955), pp. 1-50.

14. PG 31:889-1306; tr. W. K. L. Clarke, *The Ascetic Works of Saint Basil* (London: SPCK, 1925). The *Long Rules* are also tr. by M. M. Wagner in FC 9:223-337 (1950).

15. *On the Psalms*, tr. S. Hebgin and F. Corrigan, ACW 29-30 (1960-1961).

*Gospel,*[16] the *Confessions,*[17] and the less known *Soliloquies.*[18] The "contemplation" — commonly but less correctly called the "vision" — at Ostia is probably the best known text in Christian spiritual literature, but it is typical of others in Saint Augustine which have passed on, either directly or through Saint Gregory the Great, into the Middle Ages.

These reflections are being put on record by way of introducing a study of a twelfth-century writer; I have said that he finds his place between two periods, or better between two tendencies, which I have called "conceptual" for want of any better word. The first is that of the earlier Fathers, also of the Councils. Against one heresy after another popes and bishops had to come to some agreement as to how revealed truth could be safeguarded with an adequate formula. The very roughest sketch of Conciliar history would be out of place here; but we have to remember that the early centuries, especially after the so-called "peace" of Constantine, were characterized by such tensions. The *homo-usion* (consubstantial) formula of Nicaea was the most controverted and is to us the best known; but, like Gibbon, we may not know enough about it to understand how the Christian world could be torn to pieces with a quarrel over a vowel or a diphthong. The word was not scriptural, it had been condemned in the sense in which it had been used by Paul of Samosata; there was the language difficulty, and not all were using such words as *usia* or *hypostasis* (untranslatable, but quite literally 'essence' or 'substance') in the same sense. But Saint Athanasius, indeed most of the simple faithful, were in no doubt as to what was at stake: with the Fathers of Nicaea they must insist that the Son was the *same* Substance with the Father.

These then were the conditions under which the way was prepared for a meditative theology. I have called it patristic, because, from Origen onwards, it characterized most of the

16. *Homilies on the Gospel according to Saint John and his First Epistle* [tr. J. H. Newman] LF, 2 vols (1849).

17. *Confessions,* tr. J. G. Pilkington in *The Basic Writings of St Augustine,* 2 vols. (New York: Random House, 1948) 1:3-256.

18. Tr. T. F. Giligan, FC 5:333-426 (1948).

Fathers, up to the one whom Mabillon called the last of them: Saint Bernard. Here are the antecedents of one who, though far from being an amanuensis, was still a disciple of Saint Bernard; who belonged to Saint Bernard's school, but was capable of rich and original thought and expression.

This preliminary sketch is not meant to suggest that the writers mentioned had anything like a direct influence upon Guerric of Igny. For instance Saint Gregory of Nyssa and Denys the Areopagite have just been mentioned. It is remarkable how little Denys was known in the West, even though translations of his works were available.[19] If there is the least direct influence upon Guerric, it has escaped me. It may be enough to read the place where he comes nearest to a theology of darkness: "The more his lamp is enlightened, the more truly is his darkness revealed to him by the lamp itself . . . ;"[20] and then put this beside the *Mystical Theology* of Denys.[21] The writings have nothing in common.

The question of Gregory of Nyssa is not quite so simple. Daniélou has shown how Saint Bernard was introduced to Gregory's work, *On the Creation of Man*,[22] probably by his friend William of Saint-Thierry, and accordingly developed his doctrine of God's image in man.[23] The lives of William and of Guerric were so close that a similar indirect influence of Gregory of Nyssa has an a priori likelihood; but it has yet to be established from a study of his writings. In fact the very restricted image doctrine which we find in Guerric draws its origin rather from Saint Augustine.[24]

If we say that Guerric of Igny came before the scholastics,

19. Saint Bernard may have been influenced indirectly; the thought and terminology of Denys are more apparent in William of Saint-Thierry and Isaac of Stella. So André Fracheboud: *Dictionnaire de Spiritualité* III, 329-340: *Denys l'Aréopagite en Occident: Les Cisterciens*. But the author of this article — rightly no doubt — has not a word to say about Guerric of Igny.

20. Ser. 13, Third for Epiphany: 1; I, 84.

21. Dionysius Areopagite (Pseudo-), *The Mystical Theology and the Celestial Hierarchies* (Fintry, Brook: The Shrine of Wisdom, 1949).

22. PG 44:123-256.

23. J. Daniélou, "Saint Bernard et les Peres grecs" *Analecta S. Ord. Cist.* 9 (1953), 52-55.

24. *Liturgical Sermons*, Introduction, CF 8, p. lviii.

we must still remember that the scholastic movement had begun in his day. Odo of Tournai had come and gone; William of Champeaux was flourishing; Abelard had given cause for alarm; names could of course be multiplied. In the next century came the greatest of the scholastics. Saint Thomas Aquinas and Saint Bonaventure were mystics, if ever there were such, and — this is important but easily overlooked — they were steeped in the meditative theology of the centuries which had gone before them; no less Duns Scotus in the next generation. If all the scholastics had been men of such quality, there need never have been a divorce between theology and the life of the Spirit. But the divorce came about, and the reaction of the *Devotio moderna* was inevitable. The great advantage of men like Bernard and Guerric, William of Saint Thierry and Aelred of Rievaulx — an advantage for them and for us — is that they lived before that divorce. A distinction between "theology" and "spirituality" would have been incomprehensible to them.

This summary historical outline has been attempted with a view to placing Guerric of Igny in context and making it clear what is meant by speaking of him as patristic rather than scholastic.

If what has been written above corresponds to the reality; if, as would appear, there really was a divorce between theology and spirituality, and if the two have not even now been entirely reconciled, then a Guerric of Igny, who was able and content to give expression to his reflections upon revealed truth, upon the text of the Bible above all, before that divorce took place, may be expected to have a message worth delivering even to those who are living after the Second Vatican Council.

# CHAPTER TWO

# GUERRIC FOR THE NINETEEN—SEVENTIES

TWO DEFECTS SEEM INEVITABLE in an analytic study of the kind now proposed: first that justice will not be done to the original author; secondly that he will be unduly flattered.

In the first place it will seem that his real thought and mentality are being betrayed. Whatever is said about him will be grouped under some such heading as: 1) Incarnation, 2) Redemption, 3) Sanctification. But he does not analyse his thought or split it up in this sort of way. If he speaks about the Incarnation or the Birth of Christ, his thought about our Redemption and Sanctification are there already. Take a short sentence like this: "The child is born to renew us, he who as God is born eternally to give beatitude to the angels."[1] How much is found there: the birth of Christ, its purpose our renewal, the angels in relation to him, their beatitude which evidently we are meant to share. He will be talking like that most of the time.

The best way to answer the objection (if such it be) is to admit that it is all true. If any of us have had the task of organizing or teaching courses in theology, we have been well aware of it. We teach the theology of our Redemption; sanctifying grace is there, and grace comes to us in baptism. But can we do away with the distinction between separate treatises on Redemption, grace and the sacraments? How far can we separate? To what extent can we unify? As for Guerric,

1. Ser. 6, 1st for Christmas, 1; I, 37.

the present task is to arrange and to synthesize, to put in synthetic form things which he never conceived or expressed synthetically himself. It will be difficult to comment upon the many quotations from his sermons which are to follow, because so many aspects of revealed truth will be there together. Yet it is legitimate, and to some it may be helpful, to call attention separately to the outstanding elements in his theological and spiritual thought. His mind has a store of ideas; the most important of these will appear by his emphasis and repetition. These are to be set in due order and relation. The purpose is not to improve upon Guerric, but to present him to our contemporaries. So the difficulty, which must be acknowledged from the outset, is simply this: a book about Guerric is not the same as Guerric himself.

On the other hand, will the representation of him be inaccurate in the sense that it will be unduly flattering? Yes, it usually is so with any study of an ancient or mediaeval writer presented to men of the present day. Those aspects of an Augustine, a Bernard or a Guerric, which are developed and emphasized, are those which, it is hoped, will arouse the interest and attention of contemporary readers; those which seem to stand in some relation to present day theological discussion. Many other aspects or themes — in fact hundreds of columns in the Patrology — have to be left aside. Those of us who have worked for a Lectionary have found it difficult enough to find reasonably short passages appropriate and sufficiently well contained for the purpose; and when we have found them, it has been necessary to omit phrases and whole sentences. So there is a danger that the reader of a study may turn to the original author and be disappointed.

This point is made quite frankly from the beginning; for it would be a mistake either to turn a study of this kind into a panegyric, or to suggest that Guerric had just the solutions needed for our present-day problems. It would be difficult to recommend him as spiritual reading for all Christians without qualification or distinction. Here then are one or two examples of Guerric in his working-day clothes, not dressed up for a modern reader.

One wearisome feature, especially in the years after Vatican II, is his seizing every opportunity to launch out into anti-Semitic diatribe. If this is prominent in our own author, it is certainly not peculiar to him, for he has it in common both with his contemporaries and with the patristic tradition before him.

We are in the joy of the Christmas liturgy, contemplating the One who dwells in unapproachable light, wrapped in swaddling clothes and lying in a manger. Immediately the Jews are named, a wicked and adulterous generation who contradict this sign given for their salvation. The threshing floor has been soaked with dew, but they are the fleece which has stayed dry; the plant which God's providence raised up over Jonah's head has withered, but Nineveh is saved; the loss of the Jews is the enriching and salvation of the Gentiles. So it goes on, and it seems that Guerric will never tire of it. Finally he comes to the harlots awaiting Solomon's judgement:

> The evil harlot in her rivalry would rather the baby were killed than given to me alive. But the judgment of our Solomon, whose word is more piercing than any two-edged sword, searching minds and hearts, made no mistake in finding the mother. "Keep the baby alive," he says, "give him to the Church. She is his mother."[2]

Saint Bernard has already concluded a sermon for Christmas Eve by addressing the "heartless Synagogue" and recognizing in her the harlot who would rather have the child cut in two with a sword than given over to her rival.[3] Both have learnt this from Saint Jerome.[4]

There will be occasion later to speak more fully of a theory of the Redemption, which is not Guerric's own, but is taken over by him and his contemporaries from a tradition going as far back as the second century. It was essential that by all means the Incarnation of the Son of God should be kept

2. Ser. 8, Third for Christmas: 2-4; I, 50-52.
3. St Bernard, Christmas Eve 6, n. 11; *The Nativity* (Scepter Press, 1959), p. 60.
4. St Jerome, Letter to Rufinus; PL 22:682-5.

secret from the devil; for he would know that, if he went
beyond his rights in attacking God, he would lose rights
which he had acquired over man. He swallowed the bait
which was the Manhood; he found his jaws pierced with the
hook which was the Godhead of Christ. His rights over man
were lost for ever.[5]

This is not so much a criticism of Guerric, as a frank re-
cognition that he belongs to the twelfth century and not to
the twentieth. We have no genius here who will mark the
beginning of a new epoch in theology; but we have a faithful
witness to the best that has gone before him; a witness also to
less attractive elements and those which Tradition will quietly
lay aside. (It is true that it has taken the Church rather a long
time to drop the last expressions of anti-Semitism.) Thus to
draw attention to aspects of the patristic heritage which are
of little value to us is only honest and realistic. This acknowledgement made once and for all, there will be no need to
repeat it.

Is it not short-sighted to put an author back on the shelf
because he does not conform to the very latest standards,
which in any case are likely to be out-dated next year? One
whose reading is selective in this way will be restricted not
only to the century, but to the decade, if not to the year, in
which he is living. To read the works of one who wrote in an
age very different from our own demands patience and perse-
verance; but he who is unwilling to exercise these student's
virtues will never have a sense of Christian Tradition. It is
essential that there should be a process, and a laborious one,
by which the eucalyptus is extracted from the bark of the
tree. If this is seriously undertaken, it will be richly rewarded
in the long run.

There are, then, two defects, which it is difficult to avoid in
a study which is analytic: betraying the author's thought and
flattering him unduly. Yet the study has to be attempted
with all its hazards, if Guerric of Igny is to be allowed to

5. Ser. 30, 2nd for Palm Sunday; 2, 3; II, pp. 60-61. See commentary, with
parallels in chapter 9, below, pp. 105-130.

make his contribution to theology as we understand it today. The undertaking will have justified the time and effort involved, if a few readers are drawn to a meditative reading of the author's own pages.

# CHAPTER THREE

# THE UNITY OF GUERRIC'S WORK

THERE ARE TWO POSSIBLE WAYS of viewing this collection of fifty-four sermons. In the first place, thinking of a "sermon" as we understand it today, we may think that these were preached in the monastic chapter as occasion demanded, without any idea of one sermon leading to another or standing in relation to it. Records of some kind (*tabulae* or *quaternuli*) were kept. The day came when the preacher, or perhaps someone else, decided that they could be put together to furnish a volume. But this was a collection of quite distinct pieces. Such a thing could easily have happened, not quite so easily now, but certainly in the early part of our century.

To account for Guerric's sermons in this sort of way would be an outstanding example of imposing our present-day mentality upon something which happened eight centuries ago.

On the other hand, the so-called "sermons" may have been compiled as a single book. If this happened, we should expect to discern some progress in the author's thought going all the way through.

We must ask whether some such unity is discernible in Guerric's work, i.e. some progress in his thought, which would support the idea of a book conceived as such. The supposed unity is not merely redactional, but it is genetic, arising from the very nature of the work and its origin. It consists in, and is shown by, such a progress and development. I confess that the idea has come to me at a late stage, so that I am not answering this question as well as might be done. I can justify myself by the principle that, if we have got so far only as to ask the right questions, we have done something.

My idea of the sermons as a single work began to be clarified when I investigated the scriptural quotations: an exercise in elementary arithmetic of which some account will be given in the next section. This probability needed of course to be reinforced with considerations of a deeper kind. As for what I say now — I hesitate to give it even the name of an hypothesis, but it is certainly a possibility which might be investigated in a further study. One may be able to show that Guerric's knowledge and use of the Bible are gradually developed throughout this corpus of sermons. At Advent he uses more than anything else the Psalms, which are very familiar to him from his daily singing of the Divine Office; he also quotes the Proverbs as though he were carrying them in his head. At Christmas, Epiphany and Purification, he is, one might say, spoon-fed on the Gospel texts which the Church puts before him. Two new characteristics appear in the sermons on Saint Benedict. The Epistles have often been quoted, as they always will be, and those to the Corinthians more than any others — the author seems to know the First Epistle by heart. But now, and again on Palm Sunday, the letter to the Romans is used as never before, being quoted more often even than those to the Corinthians. Again, it is in these same three sermons on Saint Benedict that the Wisdom literature is used more than hitherto. At Easter there are commentaries on texts which are not so clearly indicated by the Liturgy of the day as were those in the Christmas cycle. Two of the sermons on Saints Peter and Paul carry us far from the feast of the Apostles; they are a profound treatise in mystical theology, based on a text of the Song of Songs: . . . "until the day breathes and the shadows flee."[1] In the second sermon of Our Lady's birthday we arrive at what may be Guerric's most important contribution to spiritual theology: the

---

1. Song of Songs 4:6.

middle form between the two *forms* of Christ, of God and of a servant:[2] "the form, that is to say, of the life he lived in his body, to 'form' those who were to believe in him;"[3] then the active part played by the Mother of Christ in this "forming" (*informatio*).[4]

These, then, are some of the elements which have suggested a gradual development of the author's reading and thought throughout a series of sermons which may have been compiled over a course of years.

From whatever point of view an author is studied, there is usually a proliferation into *ifs* and possibilities, so that one hypothesis will suggest the next one that has to be explored. If it can be established that Guerric's thought developed gradually through the sermons, it seems to follow that they were compiled as a book in the order in which we have them. The historical value of the *Magnum Exordium* is slight enough; but here is the text: "He remembered the book of Sermons which he had made. . . . I mean the book of sermons, which I dictated at your request."[5] This by no means excludes the supposition that the substance of the sermons was delivered in the community Chapter; indeed the phrase, "which I dictated at your request," is most easily understood if the monks asked to have permanently recorded something which they had heard. This is all in the context of the burning of the manuscript of sermons. Whatever be the value of the story, it speaks again of "such spiritual sermons . . . which he gave in community Chapter on the chief solemnities".[6]

It is possible then that Guerric's sermons, as we have them, were written as a book. Jean Leclercq argued in favor of some sermons of Saint Bernard having been compiled simply in this way, perhaps never actually preached, particularly the

2. Phil 2:6-7.
3. Ser. 52, 2nd for Our Lady's birthday: 1; II, 199.
4. Cf 8, Introduction, *Liturgical Sermons,* pp. xxxi-xxxv.
5. *Exordium Magnum* p. 166, 3-9.
6. Ibid. p. 164, 26-29. These considerations are appended to what had been said already about Guerric as preacher or writer: CF 8, Introduction, pp. xviii-xxiii.

*Sermons on the Song of Songs.*[7] He was supported by manuscript evidence of a long process of re-arrangement and revision. There is no such evidence in the case of Guerric; at least it is the opinion of the editors that the changes made in the "Middle" recension come from Clairvaux, not from Igny, and so not from Guerric.[8] But the character of the sermons as a book might possibly be established by considerations intrinsic to their doctrine: in fact to an increasing understanding and ever more developed use of scriptural texts. However there is one pertinent consideration which does arise from the manuscript evidence. In the early stages of editing we meant to establish the text of all the seasonal sermons for a first volume in *Sources chrétiennes.* Those for the Saints, beginning with Saint Benedict, would have formed a second. One possible advantage might have been an Introduction appropriately designed for each. Dom Leclercq did not approve of this, and persuaded us to keep the sermons in the order which they have in all known manuscripts. If the sermons were written together and designed as a book, it is easier to understand that — apart from a few late manuscripts which give single sermons — they should always have been written together in an order which never varied.

These few considerations may not be out of place; for theologians sometimes pass mistaken judgments through not fully appreciating the *genre littéraire* of what they handle. Without this appreciation the value and meaning of what lies hidden in our sources is almost bound to escape us.

It is one thing to follow the possible development of Guerric's thought throughout the sermons; another to confine ourselves to one aspect of theology (what in later days we have come to call theological "tract"), and to give a synthesis of Guerric's Christology with its implications for us. It is the latter task, not the former, which is being undertaken here, though within modest limits.

---

7. Leclercq, Introduction, *The Works of Bernard of Clairvaux*, vol. 3, CF 7.
8. SCh 166:77.

# CHAPTER FOUR

## SCRIPTURAL TEXTS

IT GOES WITHOUT SAYING that Guerric's chief source is the inspired word. We expect, too, that he will express himself most often in the phrases of the Psalter which, as a son of Saint Benedict, he sings every week. Here is the result of our investigations. Most of what is said—not all—will apply to other monastic writers of his period. The word "quotations" is used here in a broad sense: applied to direct quotations which can be printed in inverted commas, but also to clear reminiscences of scriptural texts. As far as possible all of these have been traced and indicated in the foot-notes of the editions (*Sources chrétiennes* and *Cistercian Fathers*). There may be no harm in giving a few statistics, provided that we recognize how much there is that statistics cannot give us. The figures have not the advantage (or the disadvantage either) of coming from a computer, or even an adding machine; they are subject to all the hazards of a paper and pencil effort.

In Guerric's fifty-four sermons more than two-and-a-half thousand scriptural quotations have been found: 2,541 to be exact. This includes repeated quotations; e. g. the important text 2 *Corinthians* 3: 18 ("We all, with unveiled face, beholding the glory of the Lord, are being changed into his likeness . . . ") is found to be quoted eight times. It follows that the number of quotations (2,541) considerably exceeds the number of texts quoted: these amount to 1,967, as appears from the scriptural index prepared for the *Sources chrétiennes* edition.

More account is being taken here of the higher figure, the number of quotations, repetitions included; for this shows us what is the average number of quotations in any sermon.

The sermons do not often differ greatly in length; and incidentally this may support the view that the text closely resembles sermons actually preached in Chapter during a limited period available in the day's curriculum. The average length of a translated sermon is a little under six pages in the format of *Cistercian Fathers Series*. Spoken aloud just as we have it, such a sermon lasts twenty or twenty-five minutes. Guerric's sermon may have lasted never more than twenty minutes, for our translations, whether into French or English, are rather longer than the Latin, the only original available to us. Of course this conjecture depends on the relation of the Latin sermon which we have to what Guerric may actually have said. We suppose always that there is such a relation; though some might question it.[1]

There are fifty-four sermons, and the number of quotations, broadly understood, amounts to 2,541. So in any one sermon of that length we may expect to find from forty-five to fifty scriptural quotations.

If these figures are to have more meaning, we must see how quotations are drawn from the different books of the Bible. This is not simply a game; it must be of interest to know what books held the largest place in the thought, memory and expression of Guerric and probably of others like him. In the five Advent sermons, considerably more than a third of the quotations are from the Psalter: 115 out of 280, while the next largest group, the Prophets, has only 51. It might have been expected that this proportion would be found throughout, but in fact the Christmas and Epiphany sermons (nine this time instead of five) have only 94 places from the Psalms and 90 from the Gospels; the five for the Purification 56 from the Psalms and 53 from the Gospels. Certainly this prominence of the Gospels is to be expected at Christmas, Epiphany and Purification; but the texts are far from being

1. Cf above p. 18, note 6, and the place indicated in the Introduction.

confined to the two Infancy narratives. In any case the increased use of the Gospels continues, and it is found in
groups of sermons where it would not so obviously be indicated. In a few groups the Gospels are quoted more often
than the Psalms. In the three Annunciation sermons certainly
this is not surprising; but we find the same in the Easter
group (three sermons), Rogation-Ascension-Pentecost (four),
also in the Assumption and Birthday of Our Lady (six),
where the use of the Gospels is not so much˙expected. One
might think that the Psalms, and still more the Prophets,
would be drawn upon for Saint John the Baptist, but the
places from these two sources together are only 37, while the
Gospels are quoted 63 times in the four sermons devoted to
John. Such variations are not simply as unpredictable as the
weather, or mere coincidence; they may possibly indicate a
movement in Guerric's thought and give some clue as to how
the sermons were compiled.

It is not surprising that the Prophets are used more than the
Gospels in Advent. In the remaining sermons of the Christmas cycle they are used rather less; in Lent again rather more.
The only other two groups of sermons in which they are used
more than the Gospels are the four sermons for Saint Benedict, and also, rather surprisingly, the three for Saints Peter
and Paul. It was not surprising to find that Isaiah was used
more than any prophet in Advent; he was also to be expected
at Christmas and Epiphany. At Christmas alone there are 45
citations from the Prophets, of which 35 are from Isaiah; this
is explained only in part by the frequent use of *Puer natus est
nobis.*[2] This prominence of Isaiah was not expected to continue after Christmas and Epiphany, but in fact it does. Here
are a few less expected proportions of Isaiah in the prophets:
9 out of 16 in Lent; 13 out of 28 in the Passion sermons of
Palm Sunday, where Jeremiah, the prophet used in the Passion Liturgy, appears only twice; 7 out of 11 at Easter; 6 out
of 13 at Rogation-Ascension-Pentecost; 18 out of 23 at the
Birthday and Assumption of Our Lady. It was to be expected

2. Is 9:6.

that there should be a high proportion at the Annunciation, where in fact Isaiah is found 23 times out of 31. In the four sermons for Saint John the Baptist one would look for something of Jeremiah and Malachi. The Prophets are used 24 times; Jeremiah is quoted 6 times, Malachi 5, but Isaiah 10. Probably in all periods and for most readers of the Bible, Isaiah has been the best known and the most used of all the Prophets. (A biblical scholar might say at once that he has an advantage over the others in being at least three authors instead of one.) As for Guerric — in every group of sermons Isaiah is used the most often, sometimes more often than the rest put together.

Of the Gospels Matthew and Luke are the most used, Mark is used little and John less than one would expect. Of course Luke is prominent in Our Lord's Infancy. The use of John is hardly noticeable until we come to the sermons on Saint Benedict, and even here he is found only 11 times out of 27. He appears slightly more than either Matthew or Luke in the Resurrection-Rogation-Ascension-Pentecost sermons; one could indeed have expected to find him more often in these last Mysteries.

By the "Epistles" is meant Saint Paul's letters to the churches, the Pastoral and Canonical letters, also that to the Hebrews. These are the only other group of books used so much as to call for any comment. The Epistles appear less than the other groups in Advent; but in the Christmas and Epiphany sermons the lists of quotations are: Epistles 142, Psalms 94, Gospels 90, Prophets 75. The only other sermons in which the use of the Epistles prevails over the others are the four for Saint Benedict. However they are always much used, and in the fifty-four sermons taken together they have the highest total after the Psalms. By far the greater number of these places are taken from the letters to the churches; the others (Pastoral, Canonical and to the Hebrews) are little used.

It is interesting to see that Guerric uses the two letters to the Corinthians more than any others. Is he afraid of the very difficult teaching on original sin and justification in Romans? In the quotations from the Epistles, those from Corinthians are sometimes half or more. Beginning with Advent, we find 11 out of 20; at the Purification there are 21 out of 33. The letter to the Romans is not prominent before the sermons on Saint Benedict; here, out of 37 Epistle quotations, 13 are from Romans and 11 from Corinthians. This group and the four for Palm Sunday are the only ones in which Corinthians has not a majority; but Romans continues to have more prominence than formerly. On Palm Sunday there are 9 places from Romans and 8 from Corinthians; but the use of Corinthians here has an interesting feature. At the beginning of the second of the four sermons the author quotes in succession four places from the first and second chapters of the first to Corinthians. He begins with 2:2 and 2:6-7, but the other two places are from the first chapter and much more widely spaced in the letter. This, together with the prevailing use of Corinthians almost throughout, gives reason to suspect that Guerric has memorized at least the first letter, perhaps the second also.

So much for the four main groups from which Guerric quotes: here they are in the order in which they prevail and with the total of quotations from each: Psalms 566, Epistles 532, Gospels 528, Prophets 368. So there is not a very notable difference between the use of Psalms, Epistles and Gospels; the two latter are virtually the same, and might indeed be reversed in someone else's counting.

The 513 quotations which remain are so dispersed that no part of the Bible seems to invite much comment. There was a first impression that the Proverbs were often quoted; but there are only 22 quotations in the Advent sermons, and the book appears but little afterwards. There are quotations from the rest of the Wisdom literature, but surprisingly few. These books are hardly noticeable until we come to the four sermons for Saint Benedict, which have 12 places from Sirach, 11 from Wisdom, 10 from Proverbs and 4 from Ecclesiastes: 37 in all, a little more than either the Prophets or the Gospels. The Song of Songs appears less than one might expect. In the three sermons for Saints Peter and Paul it is quoted ten times, but this is partly due to repetition, and will be further explained. It is found 17 times in the six sermons of Our Lady's Assumption and Birthday.

We may be surprised how little Genesis is used, or any part of the Pentateuch. Genesis is prominent only in the first sermon for Easter; this is because the theme of the sermon is the old man Jacob, who has found that his son Joseph is alive in Egypt. Joseph may be fresh in the memory, because his story has been read and responsories have been sung in his honor during Lent: "Remember that it is Paschal time. Are you going to feed us with Lenten fare again?"[3] References to other single books of the Pentateuch throughout Guerric's sermons would hardly go into double figures. On the next page are the figures and the totals which may give some idea of the distribution of scriptural quotations throughout the sermons.

These statistics may be informative up to a point. By themselves they would be not only inadequate but misleading. Above all must one distinguish between a scriptural phrase which presents itself to the author's mind in passing, and a text which receives a long and exhaustive commentary. References to the Psalms are very many, but most often these are in the author's memory, come naturally as the expression of his thought for the moment and then are left aside. On the other hand there may be a text on which the author dwells at length; it may be even the opening text and the theme of a whole sermon. Four sermons only do not open with a text from Scripture: fourth for Epiphany, first for Assumption, and first for Pentecost. Neither does the Second for Lent (i.e. for the Saturday of the second week); but the whole sermon is a meditation upon the parable of the Prodigal Son. The first for the Assumption begins: "Come, my chosen one; I will place my throne in you." I know this only as an antiphon in the Office for Holy Women. However, scriptural texts sometimes assume unrecognisable forms in their laborious and varied history. It may be that those words come from a verse of the Bible, or from several combined.

3. Ser. 33, 1st for Easter: 1; II, 80.

## DISTRIBUTION OF BIBLE QUOTATIONS IN GUERRIC'S SERMONS

| Groups of Sermons | No. of Sermons | Ps. | Proph. | Gosp. | Ep. | Others | TOTAL |
|---|---|---|---|---|---|---|---|
| Adv. | 5 | 115 | 51 | 42 | 31 | 61 | 300 |
| Christmas Epiph | 9 | 94 | 75 | 90 | 142 | 92 | 493 |
| Purif. | 5 | 56 | 36 | 53 | 44 | 47 | 236 |
| Lent | 2 | 22 | 16 | 11 | 16 | 10 | 75 |
| Ben. | 4 | 42 | 34 | 27 | 58 | 65 | 226 |
| Ann. | 3 | 32 | 23 | 40 | 31 | 31 | 157 |
| Palm | 4 | 45 | 28 | 38 | 35 | 31 | 177 |
| Easter | 3 | 13 | 11 | 27 | 34 | 35 | 120 |
| Rog. Asc. Pent. | 4 | 40 | 13 | 42 | 38 | 34 | 167 |
| John Bapt. | 4 | 13 | 24 | 63 | 23 | 41 | 164 |
| Peter & Paul | 3 | 17 | 23 | 16 | 25 | 26 | 107 |
| Asspt. Nat. BVM | 6 | 41 | 23 | 58 | 39 | 48 | 209 |
| All Sts | 1 | 14 | 2 | 9 | 11 | 11 | 47 |
| Dev. Ps. | 1 | 22 | 9 | 12 | 5 | 15 | 63 |
| TOTAL | 54 | 566 | 368 | 528 | 532 | 547 | 2541 |

The necessary distinction between a text which is recalled in passing, and one which provides the theme for a prolonged meditation, must be applied in detail. There are surprisingly few quotations from the Wisdom literature; but this is not to say that it is little used. The books are hardly noticeable until we came to Saint Benedict. Then two of the sermons for his feast open with a text from the Wisdom of Sirach (Ecclesiasticus): "Beloved of God and men. . . . He sanctified him through his faith and meekness."[4] The same part of the Bible serves to open the second sermon for the Assumption and the two for Our Lady's Birthday, the second of these being an important sermon which might be regarded as the culmination of Guerric's work. Throughout the sermons there are very few quotations from the book of Revelation; however two sermons, the second and third for Easter, are an exegesis of a verse from this book: "Blessed and holy is he who has a share in the first resurrection; over these the second death has no power."[5] The Song of Songs is quoted less than one might expect; but there is another side to this too. The second sermon for the Assumption, written in an imaginative style which gives it a charm of its own, is based on the text: "Daughters of Jerusalem, tell my Beloved that I am sick with love."[6] The final "Sermon for arousing devotion at psalmody" may have been meant by Guerric as an epilogue to his whole work and an acknowledgement that the Bible has been his principal source. It is based on the text: "You who dwell in the gardens, friends are listening; let me hear your voice."[7] Above all the second and third sermons for Saints Peter and Paul give us some very profound mystical theology, an exposition of: " . . . until the day breathes and the shadows are lengthened." This seems to come within Guerric's ambit by accident, simply because it follows upon the words which were indicated for the two Apostles: "Your two breasts are like two fawns, twins of a gazelle, that feed among the lilies."[8]

4. Sir 45:1,4.
5. Rev 20:6.
6. Song 5:8.

7. Song 8:13.
8. Song 4:5-6.

So much for texts actually found in Guerric's writings. It has seemed worth while to classify these texts in some detail, because Guerric is typical of his age in his use of Scripture. This will still further justify the question next to be considered. Has he a method, and is he guided by any special principles, in his use of the Bible? As far as possible he must speak for himself.

# CHAPTER FIVE

# HOW TO INTERPRET THE BIBLE

THOSE WHO HAVE ANY EXPERIENCE of reading patristic commentaries on Scripture—sometimes precisely because their experience is limited—must be conscious of a difficulty which we had better face at an early stage. It is there as soon as we pick up the commentaries of Origen, and he is largely responsible for it. His interpretations seem very far away from the literal sense intended by the inspired author, and would find no place at all, would be firmly rejected from any thesis prepared at the Pontifical Biblical Institute. Indeed it should be so; there is no question here of any odious comparison or criticism. The Institute of Spirituality has one task, the Biblical another; these are not opposed, but complementary. But one can hear at once the criticism directed against the treatment of Scripture by the Fathers: "This text of the Old Testament has absolutely nothing to do with my spiritual progress; the application is phantastic and imaginary." Those who collaborated with the Consilium for implementing the Constitution on the Sacred Liturgy in preparing a lectionary were asked to leave aside any interpretations of the inspired text which seemed highly artificial, and especially speculation on the significance of numbers. Saint Augustine's famous thirty-eight years by the pool of Bethzatha were mentioned as an example of what should not be chosen.

But may it be that a prompt and wholesale rejection of allegorical interpretation, not evidently justified by the historical or literal sense, is too drastic? Perhaps this attitude is superficial, a refusal to penetrate through the crust of outer rock to the treasures which are lying hidden below. What is certain is that, if we cling exclusively to what is fashionable in the nineteen-seventies, our readings and meditations are going to be much impoverished. As soon as we contact a culture which was taken for granted seven centuries ago, or much earlier, we insist upon projecting our mentality into it, judge by norms which are considered valid in the year in which we are living now, perhaps were hardly perceived ten years ago and may have gone out of fashion ten years later. Let us make every effort we can to read a twelfth-century text with the eyes and mind of the twelfth century; then we can hope to find that it has depths of meaning which are relevant to every age.

We have some idea how allegorical interpretation became established. It was there from the beginning, especially in Egypt, where Philo the Jew was the best representative. Then Christians were faced with the problem of what to do with the Old Testament. There should have been no problem at all, since all the New Testament presented Jesus Christ as the Messiah, expected, prefigured, and foretold, in the inspired books. Yet the Old Testament presented difficulties for the simple faithful, as it does today. The Gnostics had been there, were still making their voices heard, however strongly Saint Irenaeus had refuted them; then came Marcion. The Demiurge of the Old Testament could not be the Father of Jesus Christ and the God of the New. But Origen anticipated the professions of faith made by the first two ecumenical Councils at least in this sense: one God, through his Eternal Word, was the creator of all things seen and unseen.[1] The books of the Old Testament had been meant by this God to foreshadow and to foretell the New Dispensation, the coming in flesh of his Son Jesus Christ. They had a meaning for Christians, and Origen had to do all that he could to tell them

---

1. It is true that the Discussion with Heraclides reveals Origen's formula: *duo theoi:* "two Gods." (SCh 67, 58). Really this is nothing but the formula of later theology: two persons but one nature.

what it was. If he did his best to save the faith of simple believers and to harmonize it with the inevitable speculation of the Alexandrines, it is also true that he set out to save the Old Testament.

Guerric and Bernard were continuing a tradition and maintaining a principle. We need not agree with their particular applications; but the principle cannot be disputed and has the authority of the New Testament behind it. What matters most of all is not just how they say things; whether a text has been correctly translated from Hebrew or aptly applied. Whatever artifice we find in their speech, what is essential is the spiritual value of what they are saying to us.

But is Guerric's use of Scripture governed by norms inherited from the past, which he applies naturally and as a matter of course? If so, we need to understand them; otherwise we stand little chance of perceiving what kind of theology he is giving us, or of recognizing him as a theologian at all.[2]

If his sermons have been designed as a single work, the one which is placed last of all in all the manuscripts must be regarded as an epilogue.[3] The author acknowledges his principal source, and gives an idea of the kind of thing which he has been trying to pass on from it to the reader. It is the only sermon which does not belong to a particular day in the liturgical year, and is a commentary on the verse from the Song of Songs: "You who dwell in the gardens, friends are listening; let me hear your voice."[4] Speaking as one who dwells in the grave-yard, he addresses himself to those who are in the gardens, meditating upon God's law day and night. Every book is a garden, every sentence a piece of fruit. This is fruit which is none the worse for long storage; old and new are there, the inspired word of Prophets, apostles and evangelists. We must search the Scriptures where we will find Life: Christ himself. Let us pass through this garden not like aim-

---

2. See the summary account in the Introduction: CF 8, pp. xxviii-xxx. It is difficult to avoid some repetition here.
3. Ser. 54, " . . . for arousing devotion at psalmody"; II, 213-218.
4. Song 8:13.

less wanderers, but rather like bees who will suck the honey from every flower.[5] "There is need for searching, not only to draw out the mystical, but also to taste the moral sense." "Mystical" in the old sense of the word, all that belongs to the Mystery of Salvation through Christ. "Moral" in the old sense, not merely our observance of precepts or even of counsels, but our life of union with God. Yet the two are one, for it is the Mystery which unites us to God: " . . . reap the spirit from the words."[6]

Guerric has insisted already that reading is a serious business, by no means a recreation in which we can indulge until the ringing of the next bell. "When you sit down to read and you do not really read, or if before you even begin to read you put the book down again, what good do you think that will do you? If you do not continue with the Scriptures so as to become familiar with them through assiduous study, when do you think they will open themselves to you?"[7] The three loaves demanded by the importunate friend are the three senses of Scripture, which Saint Ambrose has taken from Origen and passed on to the Middle Ages: "A fine meal can be made of the three loaves of the historical and allegorical and moral senses."[8]

There is no artificial transition from one sense to another, depending simply upon the alertness of the preacher's imagination. In another sentence Guerric is not content to enumerate the three senses, but tells us that they are closely bound together: "When Scripture relates the mysteries of our redemption, it describes the historical events enacted for us in such a way as to throw light upon our moral path."[9] The Mystery is given to us under the veil of an historical narra-

5. For this simile cf St Aelred, ser. 19, first for Our Lady's Birthday; PL 195:320.

6. Ser. 54: 2; II, 214. H. De Lubac, *Exégèse Médiévale* I, 591, n. 8.

7. Ser. 22, First for St Benedict: 5; II, 6.

8. Ser. 36, Rogation: 4; II, 102. There is of course a four-fold division which adds *anagogia*; for the implication of this in Guerric see CF 8, *Introduction*, p. xxix. For Origen, see De Lubac, *op. cit.* I, 198f. Ambrose on ps. 36, n. 1; Bernard, *On the Song of Songs* ser. 17: 8; CF 4, 132.

9. Ser. 18, 4th for Purification: 1, I, 120.

tive, and this is at the same time a norm of life for us. There is another sentence, especially dear to De Lubac, which can be appreciated in its full context:

> Now that you may know more fully that the Virgin's conception has not only a mystical but also a moral sense, WHAT IS A MYSTERY FOR YOUR REDEMPTION IS ALSO AN EXAMPLE FOR YOUR IMITATION, so that you clearly frustrate the grace of the mystery in you if you do not imitate the virtue of the example. For she who conceived God by faith promises you the same, if you have faith; if you will faithfully receive the Word from the mouth of the heavenly messenger, you too may conceive the God whom the whole world cannot contain, conceive him however in your heart, not in your body. And yet even in your body, although not by any bodily action or outward appearance, nonetheless truly in your body, since the Apostle bids us glorify and bear God in our body.[10]

If we take the last paragraph of the second Purification sermon, it may seem at first sight that there is an artificial transition from narrative to moralizing: "If now, brethren, as is usual, you would be built up in a moral way, consider the four illustrious persons in this procession. . . ." But is there anything artificial; or has anything been ingeniously thought up by the preacher? Self-denial, devotion, humility and obedience on our side, on God's side merciful love, are all there in the Mystery proposed to us. Anna fasts and prays, Simeon waits until he can embrace the Savior, the occasion of this is Mary who, owing nothing to the law, comes in humble obedience for the rite of Purification. Jesus is there as the Redeemer of all who have waited under the Old Dispensation. That these riches and any others are already in the Mystery, come from there and nowhere else — this is Guerric's final reflection: "In him are the source and perfection, not only of this virtue, but also of all the others, by him they are distributed one by one, through him they are preserved, with him they find their reward."[11]

10. Ser. 27, 2nd for Annunciation: 4; II, 44.
11. Ser. 16, 2nd for Purification: 7; I, 112.

If there is such a thing as a "theology of silence," Guerric's third sermon for the Annunciation is one of its principal documents. What is the first literal and historical sense of the vision shown by Yahweh to Ezekiel? This is for biblical scholars to decide, but the book loses at least half its value for us if we stop there. The Prophet has been taken to the door of the sanctuary which looks towards the East, and has found it closed. He is told that the Lord God of Israel has entered by that way, so that no man can pass through it. "It shall remain shut for the Prince. Only the Prince may sit in it, to eat bread before the Lord."[12] He eats the bread of the Word in silence; here is the business with which our own silence is to be occupied, for he invites us to come and sup with him. He is the one who eats as he sits in that gate — the Virgin's womb; he too is the Bread that is eaten. Here, if anywhere, are the allegorical and the moral sense bound up in one, the Mystery of Christ and the Mystery of our Sanctification: " . . . that Prince, sitting in the gate of the virginal womb, ate the bread of the Word before the Lord. That will be the occupation, if you are wise, which will keep you busy in your silence: to eat the bread of God's word before the Lord, like Mary keeping what is said about Christ and pondering it in your heart. Christ will find delight in eating this bread with you, and he who feeds you will himself be fed in you. The more this bread is eaten, the greater abundance there will be to eat; for when grace is used it does not diminish but increases."[13]

Finally Guerric insists that God's special grace must help us to penetrate the depths of meaning in the inspired word. He is in touch with a tradition, going back to the Fathers of the Desert, which makes the understanding of the Scriptures the measure of our spiritual progress. It may be worth while to transcribe a few words from Saint John Cassian:

12. Ezek 44:1-3.
13. Ser. 28, 3rd for Annunciation: 7; II, 54. This passage is cited at the moment only to illustrate the very close union of the senses of Scripture. It is at the summit of Guerric's Christology, and will be discussed on a later page. On the meaning of silence, cf Ser. 4, 4th for Advent: 2; I, 24 : "At this very time, if the depths of your soul keep a midnight silence . . . ."

So we have to use all diligence in committing the books of Scripture to memory, continually going back to them. . . . We repeat things over and over again. Our mind has been taken up with the business of memorizing these texts, so that at the time of doing this we have not been able to understand them. Later on we have been free from the distraction of looking about us and doing our day's work. In the silence of our nightly meditation especially we turn things over and get a clearer view of them. There breaks upon us an understanding of the deepest hidden meanings. In our fully waking hours we had no inkling of them; but they come when we are resting in a kind of sleep which leaves us barely conscious. The more this happens, the more our mind is renewed. Scripture will begin to put on a new face for us at the same time. As we advance, there will advance with us that newly acquired sacred understanding.[14]

The purpose of transcribing this passage has been not only to indicate a source, which Guerric is likely to have known, but also to point to a contrast. Cassian insists upon our effort to memorize, and speaks as though our ever deeper understanding were the outcome of a psychological process; although it cannot be denied that the continual need of divine grace is implied and understood. Guerric speaks of our effort too: "There is need for searching, not only to draw out the mystical, but also to taste the moral sense . . . scanning every syllable, like busy bees gathering honey from flowers, reap the spirit from the words."[15] But, when the light breaks upon us, it comes from God's good pleasure and when we least expect it. Let us indeed persevere with Jesus in the desert; when we think that he has forgotten us, he will transform that desert into a Paradise: "Then he will make your wilderness like the garden of delight . . . places in Scripture which previously seemed fruitless and dry will quite suddenly be filled for you at the blessing of God with a wondrous and spiritual abundance. . . ."[16] The disciples who walked to Emmaus under-

14. Cassian, Conf. 14:10-11; SCh 54:196-7.
15. Ser. 54, Devotion at psalmody: 2; II, 214.
16. Ser. 4, 4th for Advent: 1; I, 23.

stood little, but they met one who opened the Scriptures to them: "Run through the details of the story, and the loving meaning of the mystery will reveal itself to you, provided that it is Jesus who expounds the mystery to you, who on this day of his resurrection discussed with his disciples on the road to Emmaus the letter that kills and then expounded the Scriptures to them."[17] Then we read of God's unexpected visit: "Some of you, if I am not mistaken, recognize what you have experienced; often Jesus, whom you sought at the memorials of the altars, as at the tomb, [he is speaking of something rather like our Stations of the Cross, which the monks did in the early morning] and did not find, unexpectedly came to meet you in the way while you were working."[18] Now for Guerric, and for any writer of his school of thought, a new understanding of the Scriptures, so far from being the conclusion of a laborious speculation, is the outcome of this gratuitous privilege: "Then, too, what a consolation it will be if he joins you as a companion on the way, and by the surpassing pleasure which his conversation gives takes away from you all feeling of toil, while he opens your mind to understand the Scriptures, which perhaps you sat and read at home without understanding."[19]

17. Ser. 33, 1st for Easter: 2; II, 81.
18. Ser. 35, 3rd for Easter: 4; II, 95.
19. *Ibid.*

# PART TWO

"The Lord of Hosts Is With Us."

CHAPTER SIX

# THE WORD MADE FLESH IN MARY'S WOMB: THE CENTRAL DOGMA

**B**Y THE TIME OF GUERRIC OF IGNY a rule of faith has been established; he and his contemporaries can be in no doubt as to what is the central dogma of the Incarnation of the Eternal Word. I shall recall the dogmatic definitions which he had before him, and as far as possible shall give our author's doctrinal statement, though inevitably this will contain an element of symbol and of allegory. It was for our Redemption that the Word was made Flesh; so the quotation of a parallel text of Saint Bernard will involve an excursus into the idea of the "redemption" of the angels: what was the meaning of the Incarnation for us and for them. This purpose of the Incarnation strictly belongs to a later chapter; but it is hardly possible to exclude it here. Whatever Guerric says about the Incarnation looks to its purpose; it is for our redemption and for our renewal; this idea of renewal is very prominent in Guerric. The Incarnation has two aspects: it is utter humiliation; it is also triumph. But the very humiliation is for us a triumph; since, if Christ humbled himself, it was that we might be exalted. He chose the Virgin's womb, that we might enter the courts of heaven.

## THE RULE OF FAITH: STATEMENT OF DOCTRINE

"The Word became flesh and dwelt among us, full of grace and truth; we have beheld his glory, glory as of the only Son from the Father."[1]

1. Jn 1:14.

39

"This eternal Only-Begotten of the eternal Father was born of the Holy Spirit and the Virgin Mary."[2]

"So with the character of both natures unimpaired, coming together into one person, humility was assumed by majesty, weakness by strength, mortality by eternity; and in order to pay the debt which lay upon us, the inviolable nature was joined to the nature subject to suffering. . . ."[3]

"So the Son of God enters the weakness of this world, coming down from his heavenly throne yet not leaving the glory of his Father. He comes in a new order, born in a new birth. In a new order: because invisible in what belongs to him, he is made visible in what belongs to us. The incomprehensible would be comprehended. Existing before all time, he has a temporal beginning. The Lord of all things hides his immeasurable majesty to take the likeness of a servant. The impassible God does not disdain to become a man able to suffer, and the Immortal to subject himself to the laws of death."[4]

It is hardly necessary to apologize for quoting first from Saint John's Gospel, then from the *Tome of Leo* accepted by the Council of Chalcedon in the year 451. Guerric could have heard these passages read in the Liturgy, for they are repeated in Saint Leo's sermons.[5] In the Eastern Church Chalcedon was not the final solution of a problem; it was only the beginning of a period of bitter controversy, marked especially by the compromise of the Fifth Ecumenical Council, the Second of Constantinople, concluded in the year 553. The existence of two wills in Christ — that is two complete natures — had to be asserted by Pope Martin I at the Lateran Council of 649. He suffered martyrdom for this; yet it was almost exclusively the Eastern Church which was torn by the subsequent battle which ended only with the Third Council of Constantinople in 681. This doctrinal struggle, in which

2. *The Tome of Leo*; DS 291; TCC 247.

3. *Id.*, DS 293; TCC 248.

4. *Id.*, DS 294; TCC 249-251.

5. William Bright's translation of the *Tome of Leo* is given with cross-references to the first and second Christmas sermons (22:2; 23:2) in *Christology of the Later Fathers, The Library of Christian Classics*, vol. 3 (Philadelphia: Westminster Press, 1954), pp. 360-370.

even emperors posed as theologians, and the common people in the market-place wrangled over Greek technical terms like *usia, proposon* and *thelesis,* is very difficult for us to understand if we think of it as a doctrinal controversy and nothing more. It may have been political as much as anything else, asserting the supremacy of Constantinople, the New Rome, over such venerable patriarchates as Antioch, Jerusalem, and Alexandria.

This is not to say that the Western Church was entirely without its troubles. The Arian heresy persisted for a long time after the first two Councils, because the Goths and other barbarians had received Christianity in its Arian version.[6] Another heresy, apparently Adoptionist, had to be refuted in the Carolingian period.[7] But for the most parts the West remained united in the firm acceptance of what Peter had spoken through Leo. We cannot deny either that this Western unity had a political significance. If the barbarian tribes were to be welded into a civilization under the Carolingian Rule, if Christians were to present a united front first to Vikings, then to Muslims, they needed to be united themselves in that Faith which was the making of their civilization.

As for the passages quoted above — they indicate clearly the heritage into which Guerric of Igny entered. It is not to be expected that his doctrine concerning the Incarnation should show any new or surprising developments. Anyhow, it is in the above context that whatever he has to tell us about God made Man should be understood.

The Infant whom Simeon is exhorted to embrace is the Wisdom and the Loving-Kindness of God.[8] The old man has waited until God will show him his salvation in *vultu nostro;* he is now to have another fulness of days that he may see this same salvation *in vultu suo.*[9] These phrases (literally: "in our

6. P. De Labriolle, "L'Eglise et les barbares" in *Histoire de l'Eglise,* ed. A. Fliche and V. Martin, vol. 6 (1937), ch. 5. V. C. DeClercq, "Arianism" in *New Catholic Encyclopedia* 1:791-794.

7. E. Amann, "L'Adoptionisme Espagnol" in *Histoire de l'Eglise,* vol. 6, ch. 4. S. J. KcKenna, "Adoptionism" in *New Catholic Encyclopedia* 1:140-141.

8. Ser. 15, 1st for Purification: 3; I, 102.

9. Ser. 17, 3rd for Purification: 1; I, 113.

face," "in his own face") have been deliberately left for the moment in Latin. One of the most expressive and most often quoted Incarnation texts of the New Testament is found in Saint Paul's epistle to the Philippians: Christ Jesus was in the form of God; but he emptied himself, taking the form of a servant.[10] *Forma* is a key-word in Guerric's thought, inherited especially from Saint Augustine, and its meaning, for both of them, has been discussed at an earlier stage.[11] The meaning of *vultus* in that Purification sermon is not immediately evident; and I suggest that it means exactly the same as *forma* in the epistle to the Philippians. Simeon has looked upon God's salvation in human form; he is now to pass on to eternity, to that fulness of days in which he will see God's salvation in the form of God — from faith to the heavenly vision. The whole passage may be linked up with what has been said about *forma* in the place to which I have referred.

At this stage of simple statement of doctrine we can notice the position which Guerric maintains at the beginning of the second Annunciation sermon. We know how it was generally held in the twelfth and thirteenth centuries that a human soul did not animate the body until some time after Conception. This seems to be Guerric's meaning, when he says of the Baptist by now in the sixth month of gestation: "Although the power of nature had as yet scarcely finished imparting his soul."[12] In modern times the idea of simultaneous conception and animation has prevailed almost universally. Whether or not we are convinced of this; what about Christ? Christian tradition — indeed the magisterium — has recognized an exception here — if it is an exception. Guerric preaches on the feast of the Annunciation; it was at the meeting of Mary and the angel that God was made Man. "Today the Word was made flesh and began to dwell among us." He speaks of a "rule of sound faith" and of "the definition of the Church's doctrine."[13] The Church holds without any doubt that

10. Phil 2:6-7.
11. CF 8, *Introd.*; I, pp. xxxi-xxxiv.
12. Ser. 40, 1st for St John Baptist: 2; II, 124.
13. Ser. 27, 2nd for Annunciation: 1; II, 39.

Christ's flesh was not conceived, did not exist, before its assumption by the Word of God. The Incarnation and the conception of flesh in the virgin's womb were simultaneous. This is not to say, of course, that the animation of flesh with a human soul and the Incarnation of the Word are the same thing; but here one implies the other. The Incarnation means the assumption of our human nature, soul and body.

It is not easy to say precisely what document Guerric has at hand, or in his memory, when he speaks of a *regula sanae fidei*, according to which Christ's flesh did not exist before the Incarnation. In a letter which was read to the Council of Ephesus Saint Cyril of Alexandria denied that the Virgin gave birth to a mere man, upon whom the Word of God then descended. Against the supposed teaching of Origen the emperor Justinian drew up a list of canons, one of which denied that the body of Christ was first formed in the Virgin's womb, afterwards united to a soul and to the Word of God. This was published by a Synod of Constantinople in 543, and seems to have been approved by Pope Vigilius.[14] Guerric certainly knows a sermon on Our Lady's Assumption, written probably by Paschasius Radbertus, and circulated under the name of Saint Jerome, where very strong insistence is laid upon the simultaneous conception and Assumption by the Word.[15] Therefore, Guerric says, it was on this very day that Wisdom began to build for herself the house of our body in the Virgin's womb. But now, characteristically, he has passed from the solemn dogmatic statement to the richness of imagery; we leave this sermon for the moment.

The fifth Purification sermon opens with the following text, which may have a dogmatic significance: "When the days of purification were completed, they took Jesus to Jerusalem."[16] The manuscripts are unanimous in not com-

14. DS 251, 405.
15. "... at the moment, when the Word was made flesh from the flesh of the Virgin, the substance of godhead and manhood, without confusion, was united in her womb, so that one single Person was God and the man Christ." PL 30:131B.
16. Ser. 19, 5th for Purification: 1; I, 127. This is given as the 6th sermon in Migne. Our reasons for rejecting the sermon given as 5th by Mabillon-Migne were given a note in the critical edition: SC 166, 370.

pleting the scriptural quotation. None of them have "his," or "their purification," as the Vulgate and the Old Latin version. The immediate reason for this is quite evident: Guerric is quoting from a responsory used in the Cistercian Office. Why does the responsory depart from the known Latin versions? This is only a conjecture: "his" or "their" was perhaps omitted deliberately, because it had given rise to another error of Origen. The Alexandrine used it to maintain that Christ himself had need of a certain purification, because he had a body.[17]

FOR US AND FOR THE ANGELS: FOR THEIR REDEMPTION?

Many of these sermons in the Christmas cycle have a richness of expression, such that it is difficult not to quote them *in extenso* rather than analyse their teaching. The beginning of the first Christmas sermon is an example. It may be quoted more fully on a later page; here for the moment is a single sentence, which raises a doctrinal question. The author has spoken of the ever new and timeless birth of a Word from the Father:

> But this birth in time is new in another way, in that the Child is born to renew us, he who as God is born eternally to make the angels blessed. The eternal birth certainly is more full of glory, but the temporal more lavish in mercy.[18]

This Child was born in time for our renewal; he is the same who was born in eternity for the happiness of the angels. We recall at once Saint Bernard's teaching on their redemption. This is not explicit in Guerric, but he seems to have it in mind, when he writes: "The Child is born to renew us, he who as God is born eternally to make the angels blessed." This is, in a very few words, what Bernard has to say about the redemption of the angels in his twenty-second sermon on the Song of Songs. The one who redeemed fallen man by raising him up, redeemed also the angel by giving him the grace to stand firm. Obviously Bernard has departed from

17. Origen, 14th homily on Luke; SCh 87:220.
18. Ser. 6, 1st for Christmas: 1; I, 37.

any strict or technical sense of the word "redeem." Was it
then the Child Jesus who redeemed the angels? Yes, it was he
who redeemed them, but not as a child, not as the Word
made Flesh. As the Word with God he was wisdom right-
eousness, sanctification and also redemption for the angels.
Whatever he was for the angels, he became also for us; but to
be this for us he became the Word Incarnate, the Son of
Mary. We have other evidence that Guerric followed these
sermons of Bernard closely.[19] Bernard's passage, just referred
to, needs to be read carefully; although rather long, it is
worth quoting:

Just as he was the Word in the beginning, but was the Word
with God only, and was made Flesh that he might be also
the Word with men; in the same way, he was in the
beginning Wisdom and Justice and Sanctification and Redemption, yet to the angels only. The Father made him all
these things, that he might be such to men, and he carried
out the Father's plan. The Apostle says: "Who was made
for us the Wisdom of God." He does not say simply: "Who
was made Wisdom"; but: "Who was made *for us* Wisdom."
He was now made for us, what he already had been for the
angels.

But you may say: "I do not see how he was redemption to
the angels. For there seems no authority in Scripture for
saying that they were ever captives to sin or subject to
death, so as to have need of any redemption — putting
aside those who fell by pride and put themselves beyond all
redemption. So the angels have never been redeemed; some
not needing it, others not worth redeeming; some because
they never fell, others because they were past redemption.
How then can you say that Christ our Lord was redemption
for them? " My answer will be short. He who lifted man up
after his fall, gave the angel strength not to fall, raising man
up from his captive state, preserving the angel from falling
into it. In this way he was equally redemption for both,
setting one free, keeping the other always free. It is clear
then that Christ the Lord was Redemption to the holy

---

19. " . . . our Master, that exegete of the Holy Spirit, has planned to speak on
the whole of that nuptial Canticle, and from what he has already published has
given us the hope. . . ."—Ser. 48, 3rd for Peter and Paul: 1; II, 160-161.

angels, just as he was Justice, Wisdom, and Sanctification. Nevertheless he was made these four things for the sake of those men who can see the invisible things of God only in so far as they are understood by the things that are made. So then everything that he was for the angels he was made for us.[20]

In the passages compared there is rather more than a difference of words. Guerric's whole concept, at least here, is rather different from Bernard's, so that the word "redemption" is out of place for him. When Bernard speaks of "redemption," he is thinking of preserving from a possible fall and leading to blessedness. For Guerric "redemption" means rather paying a penalty incurred, rescuing the one already fallen. With his long training in the schools, he appreciates the meaning of "redemption" more readily than Bernard, disciple though he is. This chapter is not the one in which to discuss Guerric's teaching on redemption in the stricter sense of the word.

Yet in other respects we have a resemblance between quotations from the two authors which is too striking to be a mere coincidence. Here is the beginning of Guerric's third Christian sermon:

"A Child is born of us." For us indeed; not for himself, not for the angels. He was not born, I say, for himself. This birth did not confer being upon him, did not bring him any improvement in his condition. Before he was born in time he existed from all eternity, and was his own perfect beatitude. For he was born perfect God of perfect God. He was not born for the angels. Those who were faithful to the truth did not need redemption. Those who fell were beyond redemption. Therefore he does not make himself the angels' champion, no sign of that; it is the sons of Abraham that he champions. Born as God for himself, he has been born as a child for us, leaving himself behind as it were and skipping over (*transiliens*) the angels. Coming all the way to us, he has become one of us and, emptying himself out, made less than the angels, he has become our equal. Born in

20. St. Bernard, SC 22:5-6, OB 1:132;CF 7.

eternity he was beatitude for himself and for the angels; born in time he has become redemption for us, for we alone were the ones he saw burdened with the ancient condemnation arising from our birth.[21]

This in turn sends us straight back to yet another sermon of Bernard, the third "On the Praises of the Virgin Mary":

> A Child is born to us, a Son is given to us." "To us," not to himself; for he who before all ages was much more nobly born of his Father needed not to be born in time of his Mother. Nor was he born and given to the angels. They who possessed him in his greatness did not require him in his lowliness. To us then he is born, to us he is given, because by us he is so greatly needed.[22]

Guerric's striking phrase in the last sermon quoted — "leaving himself behind, as it were, and skipping over (*transiliens*) the angels" — points directly again to Bernard's fifty-third sermon on the Song of Songs. The theme is richly developed in a paragraph of some length; it must suffice here to pick out the words of Bernard which best illustrate the relationship:

> So he leaped (*saliit*) on the mountains, that is on the highest orders of angels. . . . He skipped over (*transiliit*) the hills also. For, as we are told, he does not make himself the angels' champion; it is the sons of Abraham that he champions. . . . In this way, then, did he leap (*saliit*) on the mountains and skip over (*transiliit*) the hills, when he deigned to make himself lower than the lowest as well as the highest of the heavenly spirits. He subjected himself not only to the heavenly spirits, but even to those who dwell in houses of clay, skipping over (*transiliens*) himself as it were, and with lowliness conquering the lowliness of men.[23]

### CHRIST MAKES ALL THINGS NEW

Another theme is running all through Guerric's first Christmas sermon: that of renewal — indeed cosmic renewal. Here

21. Ser. 8, 3rd for Christmas: 1; I, 47.
22. St Bernard, On the Praises of the Virgin Mary 3:3; OB 4:45; CF 43.
23. St Bernard, SC 53:8; OB 2:100-101; CF 31.

is the Ancient of Days. He is the one who, even without his
temporal birth, makes all things new; everything created
becomes new in so far as it draws near to him. Why has he
now been born in time? Simply for the renewal of us men:
"The Child is born to renew us."

"Unto us a Child is born." A Child who is the Ancient of
Days. Child in bodily form and age; Ancient of days in the
Word's eternity past understanding. And though, as the
Ancient of days, he is not a child, still he is always new;
indeed he is just as new as newness itself, which remains
always in him and renews all things. Every single thing
grows old just so much as it recedes from him, and is
renewed in the degree that it returns. And in a way unheard
of, the reason for his youth and his age is one and the same,
for his eternity has no beginning in birth nor decline in old
age. For him, his very newness is ancient and his antiquity
new. But in another way the newness of this temporal birth
is that the Child is born to renew us, he who as God is born
eternally to give blessedness to the angels. The eternal birth
certainly is more full of glory, but the temporal more lavish
in mercy. I was besieged by misery, misery I could not
expiate.[24]

When we come to speak of our Redemption, of the Redemption applied to ourselves, that is our Sanctification, we
shall find it conceived and expressed most often as renewal.
We are renewed because we have our innocence restored. The
entire human race, indeed our world, is on the way of becoming what it first was, what in God's design it should always
have remained. In Guerric's paragraph just quoted we can
hear once again the voice of Saint Bernard. We have with us
something always new, never old because never ceasing to
bear fruit. This New Man cannot grow old; he is the Holy
One who cannot see corruption. If we speak of his temporal
birth, let us not say that he *was* born. Rather, in the words of
the Martyrology, on which the Abbot of Clairvaux is com-

24. Ser. 6, 1st for Christmas: 1; I, 37. The theme of renewal is classical, and of
course scriptural: cf. 2 Cor 4:16; Eph 4:23; Col 3:10. "When the Lord came,
what did he bring that was new? Understand that he brought fullness of renewal
by bringing himself." St Irenaeus, *Against Heresies* 4, 31, 1; SCh 100:846.

menting, he *is* born (*nascitur*). It is a birth which is always bringing about a renewal, not in himself but in us.

Something that is always new for it always renews the mind; never old, never withering away, for it never ceases to bear fruit. Here is the Holy, to which it belongs not to see corruption. This is the New Man, never able to grow old, bringing even those whose bones are the worse for age to a real newness of life. So in today's announcement, so full of joy, with good reason, as you may have noticed, he is said to be born now, not to have been born in the past: "Jesus Christ, the Son of God, is born in Bethlehem of Juda."[25]

TWO ASPECTS of the Incarnation, of the Passion and Death of Christ, run through Christian tradition: humiliation and triumph. For centuries we have sung in the Litturgy of Holy Week, first: "My God, my God, why have you forsaken me?"[26] then: *Pange lingua*: "Sing, my tongue the glorious battle, sing the ending of the fray; now above the cross, the trophy, sound the loud triumphant day."[27] The twofold aspect finds its origin in Scripture itself, even in the recorded words of Christ. The Son of Man is to suffer; he is also to rise from the dead.[28] He comes to his own and his own receive him not; yet we have beheld his glory, glory as of the Only Begotten from the Father.[29] His soul is troubled when he comes to the hour in which he is to be lifted up on the cross and to die the death of a criminal. But at the very moment in which he is troubled, he says: "Father, glorify thy name." A voice comes from heaven: "I have glorified it, and I will glorify it again."[30] "He emptied himself, taking the form of a servant . . . ; he humbled himself and became obedient unto death, even death on a cross. Therefore God has highly exalted him." The abject humiliation has not only merited

25. St Bernard, 6th sermon for Christmas Eve, n. 6; OB 4:238; CF 10.
26. Ps 21:2.
27. Venantius Fortunatus, died 600.
28. Mk 8:31; 9:30; 10:33-34.
29. Jn 1:11, 14.
30. In 12:27-28.
31. Phil 2:7,9.

this glory; it is itself a triumph. The seer of the Revelation sees "a Lamb standing as though it had been slain"; but this Lamb is also the Lion of the tribe of Judah, who has conquered.[32] The problem of humiliation and suffering has been resolved by a humbled and suffering God.[33]

### HUMBLED THAT WE MAY BE EXALTED

"Your name is as oil poured out."[34] "Rightly, then, is the name of the God-man oil poured out, or indeed ointment emptied away."[35] The scriptural text itself is sometimes quoted with *exinanitum*: "emptied"; this comes from the Septuagint version, *ekkenôthen,* and it is to be expected that Fathers of the Church should have used it to advantage. The godhead cannot of course suffer any diminution; but the one who is the splendor of the Father's glory and the figure of his substance puts on the form of a slave.[36] Here we can see God, as it were, emptied of himself; the one who fills heaven and earth lying in a manger; the one who dwells in unapproachable light wrapped in swaddling clothes. The angelic hosts bow in awe at the sound of a voice like thunder; but now we hear the wailing of a new born child. Why? He has been emptied to fill us. He appears as though he has lost something of himself, that we may be made anew.[37]

The sermons for the Annunciation are of course much occupied with the Incarnation; but they dwell chiefly on the other aspect, the triumphant, and the privilege of the Virgin Mother, giving us just one passage on the self-emptying theme.[38] In a few pages which follow, some of Guerric's words on the humiliating circumstances of the birth of Christ, will be put beside some of those which were spoken

32. Rev 5:6, 5.
33. Cf. Dietrich Bonhoeffer, *Widerstand und Ergebung* (Munich, 1966), pp. 182-184; J. A. T. Robinson, *Honest to God* (Philadelphia: Westminster, 1963), pp. 75, 82.
34. Song 1:3.
35. Ser. 8, 3rd for Christmas: 2; cf. Ser. 16, 3rd for Purification: 3; I, 48, 108.
36. Phil 2:7.
37. Ser. 6, 1st for Christmas: 2; I, 38.
38. Ser. 28, 3rd for Annunciation: 4; II, 51.

before him. It would be impossible to set out in writing all available quotations which would serve the purpose; so it must suffice to work backwards to Bernard, Bede and Ambrose. The last of the sets of parallel columns is supremely important. In Guerric, as in all patristic tradition before him, the purpose of God's self-humiliation is emphasized: to restore man's innocence, to lead him back to fulness of life. This is especially clear in Guerric, since, among those whose texts are recorded, he gives us the clearest application to our spiritual food in the Eucharist. God has become a citizen of earth that man may be a citizen of heaven. When Saint Bernard has gone through all the details of the birth of Christ, he says succinctly: "These things are mine, I am the one served, the food is set before me, the example held up for my imitation."[39]

### MANGER – STABLE

#### GUERRIC
Ser. 8, 3rd for Christmas: 2; I, 49.

Do you wish to see God emptied of himself? See him LYING IN THE MANGER. "Behold our God" says Isaiah. . . . "Where? " I ask. "IN THAT MANGER," he says. It is an infant I find there. Do you mean to say that this is he who declares: "I FILL HEAVEN AND EARTH," for whose majesty the whole breadth of heaven is too narrow?

#### BERNARD
3rd sermon for Christmas: 2; OB 4:259; CF 10.

Christ IS BORN IN A STABLE, and is LAID IN A MANGER. Is not he the one who says: "MINE IS ALL THE EARTH AND ITS FULNESS"?

39. St Bernard, 3rd for Christmas: 1; OB 3:257-258; CF 10.

**BEDE**
Commentary on St Luke I; CCL 120:49-50.

She wrapped him in swaddling clothes AND LAID HIM IN
A MANGER. . . . HE WHOSE THRONE IS THE HEAVEN
is enclosed within the narrow space of a hard manger, that
he may give us the limitless joys of the heavenly kingdom. . . . He who sits at the right hand of the Father finds
no place at the inn, that he may FURNISH MANY MAN-
SIONS FOR US in his Father's house.

**AMBROSE**
Commentary on St Luke II; CCL 14:49.

HE IS IN THE MANGER, that you may find him at the
altar. He found no place to spare in the inn, that you might
have MANY MANSIONS IN THE HEAVENLY PLACES.

\* \* \* \*

SWADDLING CLOTHES

**GUERRIC**
Ser. 8, 3rd for Christmas: 2, I, 49.

I see a child WRAPPED IN SWADDLING CLOTHES. Do
you mean to say that this is HE WHO IS CLAD IN THE
GLORY AND BEAUTY OF UNAPPROACHABLE LIGHT,
CLOTHED WITH LIGHT AS WITH A GARMENT?

**BEDE**
Commentary on St Luke I; CCL 120:49-50.

HE WHO DECKS OUT THE WHOLE WORLD IN ITS
VARIETY IS WRAPPED IN SWADDLING CLOTHES OF
COMMON MATERIAL, that we may be able to put on the
best chosen garment. The one through whom all things
were made is bound hand and foot in a cradle, that our
hands may reach out to good works, our feet be set on the
right path.

Ibid., 51.

... Here is the sign that a Savior is born: a child, not decked out with purple from Tyre, but WRAPPED IN SQUALID BANDS ...; this means that it was not enough for him to be lowly and mortal: for our sake he took the clothing of the poor.

AMBROSE
Commentary on St Luke II; CCL 14:49

He is WRAPPED IN SWADDLING CLOTHES, that you may be set free from the bonds of death. ... For you he was weak; for you he suffered want. What you see is this baby IN SWADDLING CLOTHES; what you do not see is the same in heaven.

\* \* \* \*

WAILING

GUERRIC
Ser. 8, 3rd for Christmas: 2; I, 49.

I hear him CRYING. Is this he who thunders in the heavens, at the sound of whose thunder the angelic powers lower their wings?

BERNARD
3rd sermon for Christmas: 2; OB 4:259-260; CF 10.

His message comes to you, as one might say, in terms of flesh and blood. ... This is what the TEARS AND CRIES have to say to you. Christ WEEPS; yet not like others, or indeed not for the same reason. Their tears mean bodily desires; Christ's mean love.

AMBROSE
Commentary on St Luke II; CCL 14:50.

YOU HEAR THE WAILING OF AN INFANT; you hear not the lowing of an ox that recognizes his master; "for the ox knows his owner and the ass his master's crib."

## THE EUCHARIST

### GUERRIC
Ser. 10, 5th for Christmas: 5; I, 66.

Brethren, you also will find today an infant wrapped in swaddling clothes AND LAID IN THE MANGER OF THE ALTAR. Take care that the poverty of the covering does not offend or disturb the gaze of your faith, AS IT BEHOLDS THE REALITY OF THAT AUGUST BODY UNDER THE APPEARANCE OF OTHER THINGS. For as his mother Mary wrapped the infant in swaddling clothes, so our mother grace HIDES FROM US THE REALITY OF THE SAME SACRED BODY, BY COVERING IT WITH OUTWARD APPEARANCES, which are in accord with the economy of salvation.

### BEDE
Commentary on St Luke I; CCL 120:49.

He who is THE BREAD OF ANGELS IS LAID IN A MANGER, that we, as animals sacred to him, MAY BE REFRESHED WITH THAT FODDER WHICH IS HIS FLESH.

### AMBROSE
Commentary on St Luke II; CCL 14:49-50.

He is in the manger, THAT YOU MAY FIND HIM AT THE ALTAR.

This is the Lord, this is the manger, wherein the divine mystery is revealed to us. The people who lived without reason, like beasts among their feeding troughs, ARE NOW TO BE FED WITH AN ABUNDANCE OF SACRED FOOD. The ass, type and form of the gentiles, has known its master's crib. So it is that he says: THE LORD FEEDS ME; there is nothing I shall want.

### THE PURPOSE OF CHRIST'S SELF-HUMILIATION FOR US

#### GUERRIC
Ser. 8, 3rd for Christmas: 2; I, 49.

This is our God; but he has been emptied out in order to fill you, and he has willed to fall short of himself, as it were, in order to restore you.

#### BEDE
From places quoted above.

. . . that he may give us the limitless joys of the heavenly kingdom.

. . . that we may be able to put on the best chosen garment.

#### AMBROSE
From places quoted above.

He was a little one, he was a baby, that you might grow to full manhood. He was wrapped in swaddling clothes, that you might be set free from the bonds of death. He was in the manger, that you might find him at the altar. He found no place to spare at the inn, that you might have many mansions in the heavenly places. . . .
That poverty is my inheritance; the Lord's weakness is my strength. He chose to be in want, that he might give in abundance to all. His weeping in infancy is my cleansing; those tears have washed away my sins.

For you he was weak. . . .

For you he suffered want. . . .

It is true that Bede in general depends heavily upon earlier
Fathers, and he is at pains to make this clear; but we have not
here those places in which he quotes verbatim from Ambrose
or other writers. Guerric speaks unmistakably of the
Eucharist. The meaning of the parallels given to that particular text is more open to discussion, for they could be understood simply of God's renewing grace and the bread of the
word. They may refer to the Eucharist at least indirectly, for
they enlarge considerably upon Origen's use of the ox and
the ass.[40] Ambrose is indeed drawing upon Origen, but he is
taking much more from the text of Isaiah. It would be forc-
ing Origen's words to give them a Eucharistic significance.
More than once in the Christmas sermons, Guerric applies the
symbolism of the manger from which the animals feed.[41] It
has not seemed worth while to dwell upon the figure of the
ox and the ass, since he has little to say of them: only in the
tradition of Origen: "The ass from the nations knows in the
manger the Lord became grass for him; for all flesh is
grass."[42]

If anyone reads carefully those earlier parallel texts on the
circumstances of Christ's birth, he may well say that there is
little reason to think that Guerric borrowed from them
directly, had them before him or even knew them by heart.
But there is no intention here of demonstrating that Guerric
used some particular text. If at any time he has done this, it
is interesting to know it. But it is still more important for us
to breathe the atmosphere in which he lived and moved; to
know what he had almost certainly read or heard at some
time in his life, so that it remained vaguely at the back of his
memory — nowadays we should probably say, what influenced him sub-consciously.

The Annunciation sermons contain one passage which
dwells as much as those of Christmas on the utter humiliation

40. Is 1:3.
41. Ser. 9, 4th for Christmas: 1, 5; cf. ser. 10, 5th for Christmas: 5; I, 55, 59,
66.
42. Ser. 8, 3rd for Christmas: 4; I, 51. Cf. Origen, *Homily on Luke* 13: SCh 87,
214. The two beasts have a much fuller history behind them. This has been
demonstrated by a compilation in *Monastica* 11 (1970), 8-26: *Il bue e l'asino*.

and self-emptying of the Word made Flesh. Not only did this humiliation come before all else, but it was the greatest of all that Christ suffered. Here is the "majesty which knows no bounds" (*incircumscripta*) — this word has been a favorite since Saint Gregory the Great.[43] For nine months that Eternal Wisdom remained speechless. "Where else did he so empty himself out, or when was he seen so completely eclipsed? " On the cross he prevailed against all that the powers of evil could do, gave the penitent thief the promise of eternal happiness and with his dying breath wrung from the centurion the acknowledgement: "Indeed this man was the Son of God."[44] "On the other hand in the womb he is as if he were not. Almighty power lies idle as if it could do nothing. The eternal word constrains himself to silence."[45]

The last of those parallel texts has given words in which Guerric, with others, tells us the purpose of all Christ's self-humiliation. It is that men may be raised up from their misery and have new life. The Incarnation is something which men by themselves could never have believed or foreseen; but this very humiliation of the Son of God is a victory and a triumph — the second aspect is now appearing.

### THE INCARNATION OF THE SON OF GOD IS NOT ONLY A HUMILIATION; IT IS ALSO A TRIUMPH.

The one public triumph of the gospel is Christ's entry into Jerusalem: "Blessed is he who comes in the name of the Lord."[46] For us it is associated with Christ's Passion; but the early Cistercians, like many of their time, used it to prepare for the coming of the Word made Flesh. It is not surprising to find it recurring in the Advent sermons, since the primitive Cistercian missal had it for the gospel of the first Sunday of Advent.[47] The association remained, even though after the

43. See the study of this word and idea made by Michael Frickel, *Deus totus ubique simul* (Fribourg, 1956).

44. Lk 23:43; Mt 27:54.

45. Ser. 28, 3rd for Annunciation: 4; II, 52.

46. Ps 117:26; Mt 21:9.

47. Ser. 1, 1st for Advent: 1; I, 2. The French edition (SCh 166:92) has a note on the testimony of the earliest known Cistercian breviary, and on other traces of the use of this gospel in Advent

liturgical revision made under the name of Saint Bernard, the text was changed to those opening words of Saint Mark's gospel which introduce Guerric's fourth and fifth sermons. It is interesting to find that the first sermon has not only the words of the triumphal entry, but also a reminiscence of the chant which accompanied the Cistercian Palm procession: "Whom all the saints awaited from the world's beginning." Here is a hope fulfilled, not only for the chosen people, but for all the just who have ever lived.

The first sermon for the Annunciation is taken up with the allegorical exposition of several texts. "Wisdom has built herself a house."[48] She has built it in the Virgin's womb. Saint Augustine has said already: "Wisdom has built herself a house. . . . Here we see that God's Wisdom, the co-eternal Word, has built himself a human body in a Virgin's womb."[49] Then Saint Bernard: "This Wisdom . . . built herself a house, none other but the Virgin Mary."[50] This sermon of Bernard is entirely taken up with the Marian exegesis of the text from Proverbs For Bernard the house is the Virgin herself. Guerric follows Augustine, seeing in the house the human body which he took from her: "In her and from her he prepared a throne for himself, when in her and from her he took himself a body."[51] But Guerric's thought stays very close to that of Bernard, when he thinks of the angel's promise that "the Lord God will give to him the throne of his father David,"[52] Is not Mary herself this throne? Certainly she is for Christ a throne lifted high above all the rest of creation; he has no doubt that in her is fulfilled the word of the Psalmist: "She is 'your throne, O God, enduring for ever'."[53]

Guerric is still in line with tradition when he recalls that King Solomon made himself a great ivory throne and overlaid it with the finest gold.[54] If Solomon is a figure of Christ,

48. Prov. 9:1.
49. Augustine, *The City of God,* book 17, ch. 20: Everyman's Library (Dutton, N. Y., 1947), vol. 2, p. 174.
50. Bernard, Div 52:2; OB 6-1:275.
51. Ser. 26, 1st for Annunciation: 3; II, 34.
52. Lk 1:32.
53. Ps 44:7.
54. 1 Sam 10:18.

what about the throne?  According to Nicholas of Clairvaux, one of Guerric's contemporaries, the throne is Mary herself; he has much to say about the ivory as a symbol of chastity, and here Guerric will follow him.[55] Whether this throne is the body of Christ or Mary herself makes little difference, since his chaste body is taken from hers. Guerric — though rather tentatively this time — makes the throne Christ's own body taken from Mary. The throne was decorated with dazzling gold: that glory which the apostles saw on the mountain of the Transfiguration:

> If anyone should understand by that great ivory throne, which Solomon made for himself, the very body which our Peace-Maker[our Solomon]took to himself from the Virgin on this day, he will seem not far from the truth; for the words which follow — "he overlaid it with gold exceeding bright" — suit well enough that body which the Lord now clothes in the beauty of awesome splendor. "He overlaid it," we read, "with gold exceeding bright." If you ask the apostles, whose eyes saw him transfigured on the mountain, they will acknowledge that the gold was brighter than they could bear to look upon.[56]

Rupert of Deutz has been very near to this, even without speaking explicitly of Christ's body: "The great ivory throne, decked with gold is the majesty in which the purest of all men will come to judge; in that majesty will shine as gold the justice of the godhead."[57]

Finally Guerric sums up in a few words this idea of the Incarnation as a triumph:

> Indeed, Lord, your almighty word is good and full of consolation, coming today from the royal throne into the Virgin's womb. Even there he has made himself a royal throne. Even now he is enthroned as king in heaven, with the angelic host around him. Yet from the throne of the

---

55. Nicholas of Clairvaux, Sermon for Our Lady's Birthday; PL 144:737-8 (attributed to Saint Peter Damian).

56. Ser. 26, 1st for Annunciation: 3; II, 34-35.

57. Rupert of Deutz, On the 3rd (1st) book of Kings: 31; PL 167:1177BC. More will be said of this ivory throne with reference to Mary herself.

Virgin's womb on earth he gives comfort to those who mourn.[58]

We have not expected that a Guerric of Igny should add anything to the Incarnation dogma — passed down to his time from that of the early Church Councils — other than a richness of expression and an immediate bearing upon our lives of union with God. It is inconceivable that he should ever ask whether, in the heights of contemplation, the thought of Jesus Christ, God made man, should be laid aside. We are to be faithful to our psalmody and keep that recollection which will leave us always at God's disposal. It may be at other times altogether that God will deign to visit us, but the one who will then touch our inmost being will be Jesus Christ, the Word of God Incarnate. From all eternity he was everything for the hosts of angels. God has allowed man's sin, that his mercy may transcend it; all that the Son of God is for the angels in eternity he is now for us; but to be all this, and indeed to effect the reconciliation needed, he has become one of us. The Mystery which no theologian can ever adequately expound in human words is the meeting of God and Man. No pagan could ever have thought a meeting possible; but what has happened is more than a *rapprochement*. Without Christian revelation it was possible indeed to think and speak of a Word uttered by the Supreme Being, a Word which should be the cause and exemplar of what might come into existence on another plane. What was nonsense for the pagan thinker was the notion that this Word should ever become one of ourselves: that Someone both Creator and thing created should be at the center of all. So it was, and those who were empowered to speak with God's authority had to find the best way of giving expression to this Mystery in the language of their time. Whatever terms were current in the world of the philosophers had to be brought into service; it was most necessary that these should be rightly used. If God had done something and had revealed a truth which men by themselves could never have conceived, it was essential that it should be expressed in terms which would admit of no error or misunderstanding. The truth once formulated would

58. Ser. 26, 1st for Annunciation: 2; II, 34.

not be static, a matter for repetition and no more; for its implications could be developed without end. Human words and thought would be so inadequate that figures and symbols might best serve the purpose. We have been concerned with an author for whom the figure, the symbol, the allegory, prove the most satisfying.

Guerric of Igny carries a lighted candle in procession on the day when he recalls that Christ, this God made Man, obscurely promised and long expected, came at last to the temple of his chosen people. For him that light in the wax is the Word in human flesh.[59] On another day it is Epiphany, the feast of light.

> Look! The light which is eternal has tempered itself to the weakness of your eyes; so that he who "dwells in light inaccessible" can be looked upon by eyes which are dim and weak. See the light in a lamp of earthenware, the Sun in a cloud, God in man, the Splendor of Glory and the Brightness of eternal light in the clay vessel of your flesh.[60]

Since this great truth can be known to us only by God's revelation, it has to be believed. Faith comes by hearing; but faith in such a Mystery is not easy. The day comes when it seems that something more is offered to us. "Let us then who are already in the light through faith, go forward from it and through it toward a light which is fuller and more serene. . . ."[61] The shepherds are sent to the manger, and we are invited to go with them, to see with our eyes, to look upon and to touch with our hands the Word of Life which was from the beginning.

The Mother has taken her place with her Son throughout. Guerric, with the writers of his time, speaks so richly of her virtues, her special titles, especially the types and figures through which she is known to us, that it does not seem artificial or excessive, indeed rather necessary, to devote a special chapter to the Mother of the Word made Flesh.

---

59. Ser. 15, 1st for Purification: 2; I, 101.
60. Ser. 12, 2nd for Epiphany: 1; I, 77.
61. Ser. 13, 3rd for Epiphany: 4; I, 86.
62. 1 Jn 1:1. Ser. 10, 5th for Christmas: 1; I, 62.

# CHAPTER SEVEN

# THE MOTHER OF THE WORD MADE FLESH

IT SHOULD BE CLEAR now that a mediaeval writer like Guerric is at one with the Second Vatican Council, in that he has no idea of discussing Mary apart from the Mystery of Christ and his Church. Even though he will have sermons to preach for her principal feasts, her Birthday and Assumption, we shall find her always with her Son, whether the emphasis be on God's coming into the world or upon the work of our redemption and sanctification. In a certain sense we shall find that Guerric, like others of his time, has linked Mary's holiness even too closely to her divine motherhood, since her cleansing from original sin is placed just at the moment in which, by her free consent, the Holy Spirit comes upon her so that she conceives the Son of God.

## MARY'S FIRST SANCTIFICATION

Even in the East, where we look for the first expression of belief in Mary's Immaculate Conception, Saint John Damascene has said that the Holy Spirit came upon her and purified her at the Annunciation.[1] This, in its context, is the unmistakable meaning of Saint Leo the Great: "Whereas no mother conceives without the stain of sin, this one was purified from her very conceiving.[2] So the Venerable Bede would

---

1. John Damascene, *On the Orthodox Faith*, 3, 2; PG 94:985B. Other Eastern Fathers were understood in this sense, as has been indicated in SCh 166, 306, n. 1.
2. Leo, 2nd sermon for Christmas: 3; SCh 22:80.

understand it: "When the Holy Spirit came upon the
Virgin . . . he purified her soul from all the stain of sin; the
utmost purification which human frailty could take."[3] Our
Cistercian Fathers have not yet come to maturity, when Saint
Anselm speaks his famous sentence:

> Indeed it was becoming for that Virgin to shine with SUCH
> PURITY, THAT UNDER GOD NO GREATER PURITY
> COULD BE THOUGHT OF (*ea puritate qua maior sub Deo
> nequit intelligi*). For God the Father decreed to give her his
> only Son, whom he loved with all his heart, begotten by
> and equal to himself: so to give him that God's Son and the
> Virgin's Son should be one and the same.[4]

Whatever implications theologians may see here, there cannot
be any question of attributing either to Anselm, or to Cistercians like Bernard and Guerric, the teaching of the Bull
*Ineffabilis* of 1854. It would be out of place here to discuss
Saint Bernard's well known letter to the canons of Lyons.[5]

However, after those testimonies, chiefly to Western tradition, it is interesting to see just how Guerric expresses
himself: "If beforehand her purity lacked anything at all, she
was fully purified in this conceiving."[6] Here is the teaching
of Leo and Bede, for there is not the least doubt that "conceiving" (*conceptus*) means her active conception of her Son.
Yet there is that clause introduced by "if." The common
teaching is clear; theologians of the first rank have not yet
elucidated the idea of Mary's exemption from original sin;
the question has hardly been posed; yet Guerric seems not
perfectly sure that a purification was needed. That qualifying

3. Bede, 1st homily for Advent: 3; CCL 112:18.
4. Anselm, *On the Virginal Conception*: 18; ed. F. Schmitt, II, 159.
5. Bernard, Ep 174; PL 182:332-333; LSB, Ep 215, pp. 289-293. I gave a
summary account of my view of Saint Bernard's position in a publication *Marie et
Saint Bernard* (Quebec, 1954), pp. 52-53; though I did not know at the time of
writing that my text would be translated into French, and had no opportunity to
check the printed version. It seems to me that the main lines of what I said have
been developed with great erudition by Leopold Grill: "Die Angeblich Gegners-
chaft des Hl. Bernhard v. Clairvaux zum Dogma v. der unbefleckten Empfängnis
Marias," in *Analecta S. O. C.* 16 (1960), pp. 61-91. Ailbe J. Luddy spoilt Saint
Bernard's case by trying to prove too much: *Life and Teaching of Saint Bernard*
(Dublin, 1927), pp. 695-713.
6. Ser. 15, 1st for Purification: 1; I, 100.

phrase (supported by all manuscripts) is meaningless otherwise.

But in the fourth Purification sermon he shows no hesitation in falling into line with earlier Fathers:

> "The Holy Spirit shall come upon you and the power of the Most High shall overshadow you." This overshadowing by power from on high was Mary's true purification. . . . For mortal nature had to be purified beforehand in order to conceive God, not afterwards because it had conceived, for to have conceived the Holy of Holies is supreme sanctification, and nothing could be holier than she who was made the Mother of Holiness itself.[7]

When it was said just now that the dogma of the Immaculate Conception had not yet been elucidated, the statement was deliberately restricted to "theologians of the first rank." First there was question of celebrating a feast; then it had to be clear what was being celebrated and why. A short account has been given elsewhere of the first beginnings of this enquiry in England.[8] Both Eadmer of Canterbury and Nicholas of Saint Albans were insisting that Mary never incurred the stain of original sin.[9] Under God, the appreciation and the general acceptance of this truth had to wait for the subtlety of a William of Ware [10] and the authority of a Duns Scotus.[11] But well before this time the belief had made its way across the English channel. As for the generation or so after Guerric there were some of his fellow Cistercians who felt no reason for hesitating. Here are the words of Ogler, the abbot of Locedio in Burgundy: "Among the sons of men, small and great, there is no one so holy, no one so privileged

7. Ser. 18, 4th for Purification: 3; I, 122.

8. J. Morson, "The Immaculate Conception: early Developments in England," *Pax* 44 (1954), 148-153.

9. Eadmer of Canterbury, *On Holy Mary's Conception*; Latin text edited by H. Thurston and T. Slater (Freiburg im Breisgau, 1904). Nicholas of Saint Albans: article and edition of treatise ed. by C. H. Talbot, *Revue Bénédictine* 64 (1954), 83-117.

10. William of Ware: see X. le Bachelet, article: "Immaculée Conception," in *Dict. de Théologie Catholique* VII(1), 1061. William was the master of Duns Scotus.

11. Duns Scotus, *On the 3rd book of Sentences*, ed. Vives XIV, 162.

before God, as not to have been conceived in sin, excepting only the Mother of that Immaculate One who never sinned. . . ."[12] Four sermons on the *Salve Regina* are found among the works of Saint Bernard, written probably by a certain Bernard of Toledo.[13] Mary is addressed in these words: "You were innocent of all sin, original and actual. This can be said of none but you."[14]

I should have to apologize several times for disgressions with quotations, if I were concerned with Guerric and nothing more. In fact my aim is more presumptuous: to make a patristic study (necessarily short in relation to the matter involved) centered on Guerric — or with this mediaeval author as a starting point. Yet it may be impossible really to study such a writer unless we go well beyond his own writings; impossible to appreciate him unless we put him in as wide a theological and historical context as may be allowed by time and by the patience of the reader.

### "HE HAS LOOKED UPON THE HUMILITY OF HIS HANDMAID."

"Upon whom will I rest but the humble? "[15] Guerric quotes this text of Isaiah in the context of: "I sought a resting place."[16] These are the words of the eternal Wisdom. Can God in any sense be seeking rest? Certainly the God-Man is a wanderer upon earth, has not where to lay his head.[17] If we feed the hungry, give rest to the weary, he accepts it as done to him. [18] Is God himself in his divine nature seeking rest? For Saint Augustine it is a figure of speech; a way of saying that we find rest in him: "Let us understand that God is said to rest, when he gives rest to

12. Ogler of Locedio, *On the Lord's Words at the Supper*, sermon 13; PL 184:941C.

13. So P. Glorieux: *Pour révaloriser Migne* (1952), p. 72.

14. Bernard of Toledo, *On the Antiphon 'Salve Regina'*, sermon 4: 3; PL 184:1074C.

15. Is 66:2, as quoted by Guerric in a Vulgate reading of his time, approximate to that of the Septuagint.

16. Sir 24:7.

17. Mt 8:20.

18. Mt 25:40.

us."[19] Guerric answers: If God accepts for himself whatever we do for his little ones in this life — "I was a stranger and you took me in"[20] — how much more graciously will he accept our hospitality for his Spirit which would abide in us. "Upon whom will I rest but the humble? "

No servant ever stood before him in such genuine humility as Mary; the only one who ever excelled her in humility was her Son. It was not enough that his Spirit should live and work in her. She had such fulness of humility that she was able to receive a fulness of godhead, and that in bodily form: "No one was found like her in the grace of humility; in this fullness of humility therefore rested the fullness of the godhead, even in bodily form.[21] But in the Son it rested otherwise; for if the Mother's humility was great, the Son's was incomparably greater."[22] Guerric probably remembers here the succinct and even enigmatic sentence of the homily attributed to Saint Jerome: "The fulness of grace which is in Christ came upon Mary, yet in another way."[23] There will be much to say about Mary's virginity, but this would count for nothing without her humility, so it is worth insisting upon this in the first place. Saint Bernard has said already: "If Mary were not humble, the Holy Spirit would not have rested upon her. . . . It is evident, we have it from her own words, that she might conceive by the Holy Spirit, God "looked upon the humility of his handmaid," rather than her virginity. Clearly, if her virginity was pleasing to God, this was the outcome of her humility."[24] Indeed humility is the first condition, and in some sense the cause, of chastity, as of all virtues: "It is humility that merits the gift of chastity or charity: God gives grace to the humble. . . . Mary was full of grace; but she thought fit to glory in this alone. . . . 'God has looked,' she said, 'upon the humility of his handmaid'."[25]

19. Augustine, *On the letter of Genesis*, 4, 7; PL 34:302.

20. Mt 25:40.

21. Col 2:9.

22. Ser. 49, 3rd for Assumption: 4; II, 183.

23. Probably Paschasius Radbertus, attributed to Saint Jerome: letter 9, to Paula and Eustochium: 5; PL 30:127C.

24. Bernard, *On the Glories of the Virgin Mother*, 1:5; OB 4:18; CF 43.

25. Bernard, *Letter on the Conduct and Duties of Bishops*: 17; PL 182:821B.

Guerric follows Bernard when he says and insists that Mary's humility — just what the fallen angels and Eve lacked — is of first importance. No other creature came into this world endowed with such graces; but with these she is humble.

Since this is no false humility, Mary accepts the dignity and the function proposed to her. We cannot forget the passage in which Bernard pictures the patriarchs and the prophets, all from Adam onwards, waiting in suspense for her answer. Is this mere rhetoric? We may deceive ourselves here. We may imagine that, if Mary had declined to co-operate in the Incarnation, then God would have found another way. But would he? [26] He made man after his own image, especially by endowing him with a free will. (Perhaps Bernard's greatest contribution to the development of theology is his *De gratia et libero arbitrio.*[27]) God decreed to redeem the human race. But just as the Fall came from the free choice of a first Adam and Eve, so would the Redemption depend upon the choice of a second. Mary differs from the first Eve in that she co-operates fully. We may speculate as to what might have been; but the humble and chaste Virgin gives birth to the Son of God.

### THE FRUIT OF VIRGIN SOIL

The first man was formed of the slime of an earth which no one had cultivated. Cursed by God after man's fall, it is now blessed by the coming of a Redeemer. Mary is that untouched and untainted soil; a dew has dropped from heaven and the clouds have rained down the Just One. We can trace the idea back to Tertullian, almost the first Christian who wrote in Latin: "The earth has yielded its blessed fruit, that virgin soil, never hitherto watered by rain, nor made fertile by showers. From this earth man was first fashioned of old; Christ comes from it now, when he is born of a virgin according to the flesh."[28] Saint Augustine has followed him:

26. Cf. e. g. E. Schillebeeckx, *Mary, Mother of the Redemption* (Sheed and Ward, New York, 1964), p. 92, with a quotation of this text of Bernard in n. 1.
27. G. Venuta, *Libero arbitrio e Libertà della Grazia nel Pensiero di San Bernardo* (Rome, 1953).
28. Tertullian, *Against the Jews*, 13:11; CCL 2:1387.

"Made from the seed of David according to the flesh", as
the Apostle tells us, that is as it were from the slime of the
earth, for there was no man to work upon the face of the
earth, since no man had part in the Virgin's conception,
when she brought forth Christ. But a fountain of water rose
up from the ground and watered all the face of the earth.
The earth's face, its dignity, is rightly understood to be the
Lord's Mother, the Virgin Mary, watered by the Holy
Spirit.[29]

Rupert takes up the theme,[30] but it is developed fully and in
detail by Guerric. He must be quoted at some length, for it is
difficult to find a more remarkable insight into the mystery
of our Redemption foreshadowed in the very beginning of
Creation.

Indeed today, Lord, you did bless that earth of yours,
blessed among women. Today you did bestow the kindness
of the Holy Spirit, so that our earth might yield the blessed
fruit of its womb and, as the heavens dropped down dew
from above a virginal womb might bring forth a Saviour.
Accursed is the earth in the work of the sinner, bringing
forth as it does, even when cultivated, thorns and thistles to
the heirs of the curse. But now blessed is the earth in the
work of the Redeemer, for it brings to birth the remission
of sins and the fruit of life to all men, and frees the sons of
Adam from the doom with which their origin was cursed.
Indeed that earth is blessed which, wholly untouched, not
dug nor sown, from heaven's dew alone brings forth a
Savior and provides mortal men with the bread of angels
and the Food of eternal life. So this earth, which was not
cultivated, seemed to be derelict, but it was full of rich
fruit; it seemed to be a lonely waste, but it was a Paradise
of happiness. Truly the waste was a garden of God's de-
lights, since its fields brought forth a sweet-smelling seed,
truly a full desert from which the Father sent forth the
Lamb, the Lord of the earth.[31]

29. Augustine, *On Genesis against the Manichaeans*, 2:37; PL 34:216.
30. Rupert of Deutz, *On the Song of Songs*: 4; PL 168:895D.
31. Ser. 27, 2nd for Annunciation: 1; II, 40.

MOTHER OF MERCY

Mary became not only the instrument of God's mercy, but the *Mater Misericordiae*, the Mother of Mercy, the Mother of the One who is not only God's supreme expression of mercy, but is himself the "Mercy of God." On the feast of the Purification Simeon addressed in these words: "Hold God's Mercy tight to your breast." Then it is said of Mary: "For she is the one only Mother of Mercy All-High; so that in a wonderful way her breasts are fruitful with mercy."[32]

The *Salve Regina* was then an antiphon for the *Magnificat* in the feasts of the Annunciation and Purification,[33] but the phrase *Mater Misericordiae* was not there; the opening words were: *Salve Regina Misericordiae*: "Hail, Queen of Mercy". The Phrase *Mater Misericordiae* is found before Saint Bernard,[34] and he uses it himself at least four times.[35] It is worth while to analyse the words in their context, and to see what they mean for Bernard. He never calls Mary his Mother, and his reason for this is that the title belongs traditionally to the Church.[36] There is no exception here, for *Mater misericordiae* does not mean "Merciful Mother." The *Misericordia* of whom she is the Mother is Christ himself.

In the first Assumption sermon this is most evident: "On our pilgrimage we have sent an Advocate before us. As MOTHER OF THE JUDGE AND MOTHER OF MERCY, a powerful suppliant, she will take in hand the work of our salvation."[37] The capitals are of course my own, and the

32. Ser. 15, 1st for Purification: 3; I, 102.
33. See any manuscript or printed Cistercian antiphonary between Saint Bernard's revision of the Liturgy and the later revision made under Abbot Claude Vaussin after the General Chapter of 1684; e. g. the *editio princeps* of 1545. The text is in the manuscript antiphonary preserved in the library of Mount Saint Bernard Abbey, England.
34. E.g. *Life of Odo of Cluny*; PL 153:47B, 72AB. John Gualbert, *Homily on Our Lady's Birthday*; PL 144:761B, attributed to Saint Peter Damian.
35. Bernard, 1st Sunday after Octave of Epiphany: 4 (twice); Assumption 1:1; Sunday in Octave of Assumption: 15; CF 10 and 22.
36. K. Delehaye, *Ecclesia mater chez les Pères des trois premiers siécles* (1964), Series "Unam sanctam," 46.
37. See n. 35.

editors have not even given a capital initial to *misericordiae*. They are aware of the question of interpretation, and may well have preferred to leave it open to discussion. This may serve as a norm for the two other places, where the meaning is not so evident. Near the end of the sermon for the Sunday within the Assumption octave Bernard calls upon Mary in these words: "Now, Mother of Mercy, trusting in your heart's unfailing love, the Moon lies prostrate at your feet, calling on you with your devout supplication to be her Mediatress before the Sun of Justice, that in the light which is yours she, too, may see light. . . ."[38] The Moon, prostrate at Mary's feet, seems to be the Church. "Mother of Mercy" is balanced by "Sun of Justice." Although the symmetry is not perfect in this imagery, it is precisely because she is the *Mater Misericordiae,* the Mother of him who is Mercy, that she can plead as an advocate, and, under him, a Mediatress. The text in the second sermon for the Sunday after the Epiphany octave is clearer, since the phrase is up against another, "her most loving Son": "How often, my brethren, after your tearful petitions, must I implore the MOTHER OF MERCY to remind that KINDEST OF SONS that you have no wine."[39] A few lines later we read that she is *misericors et Mater Misericordiae*: "merciful and the Mother of him who is Mercy."

It has seemed worth while to dwell upon Bernard's use of *Mater Misericordiae,* because the words first quoted from Guerric are a very enlightening commentary on the phrase, leaving no room for futher discussion as to its meaning. The old man Simeon is asked to embrace God's Wisdom and then to hold to his bosom God's Mercy. A few lines later Mary is said to have given birth to God's Mercy, and in this sense to be the "one only Mother of Mercy All-High." Here is the passage again at rather greater length: "Embrace God's Wisdom then, O blessed old man. . . . Hold God's Mercy tight to your breast. . . . For she is the one only Mother of Mercy

38. *Ibid.*
39. *Ibid.*

All-High; so that in a wonderful way her breasts are fruitful with mercy."[40]

All this might find its place later in our study, in connection with our redemption and sanctification. At the moment Mary is being considered as the Mother of the Word Incarnate. Of course the aspects cannot be separated, and it is good to be continually reminded of this. The Holy Spirit came upon her, not simply that she might be the Mother of God, even though this was her supreme dignity. That divine motherhood was to serve a purpose: our rescue and salvation. The title *Mater Misericordiae* has claimed our attention, since it means, both for Guerric and for Bernard, Mother of the Merciful Love incarnate.

### HEWN FROM THE ROCK WITHOUT HUMAN HANDS

Christ has been foreshadowed in the Old Testament as a Rock, the Stone which the builders rejected.[41] He has been hewn, says Saint Augustine, without human hands: ". . . without any work of man, for he came from a Virgin, with no embrace of husband and wife."[42] There is more to be said than this. Mary has remained a virgin even in giving birth. This truth has been in possession since the *Tome* of Leo: "Mary gave birth to him remaining a Virgin, just as she remained a Virgin when she conceived him."[43] Before this Ambrose has expressed it as clearly as possible in his exegesis of Ezekiel's Eastern Gate: "This gate shall remain shut; it shall not be opened, and no one shall enter by it."[44] "What else is this gate," he has asked, "but Mary, closed because she is a Virgin? Mary then is the gate by which Christ came into this world. He never broke the seal of her virginity, when she brought him forth by a virgin birth."[45]

If Christ is a Rock, hewn without human hands, then Mary is a Rock, too. This figure lends itself well to the expression

40. Ser. 15, 1st for Purification: 3; I, 102.
41. Dan 2:34; Ps 117:22; 1 Pet 2:7.
42. Augustine, *On John' Gospel*, 9:15; CCL 36:98.
43. DS 291.
44. Ezek 44:2.
45. Ambrose, *Instruction of a Virgin*, 6:41; PL 16:316.

of her full virginity, and Guerric takes advantage of it. Just as the risen Christ comes from the tomb in the rock, so he comes from the Virgin's womb, leaving no trace of his coming:

> If the Rock is Christ, as the Apostle says, then the Son does not belie his origin from a Mother who herself is also called a rock. Is she not rightly styled a rock who, for love of integrity was firm in her resolve, solid in her affections, in her feelings wholly without feeling and like a stone against the enticements of sin? Is not that virginal integrity a rock, which gives birth to nothing by its own natural power, and when it does give birth by the power of God's dew, is able to remain unopened both when it admits conception and when it brings forth a child? [46]

### SOLOMON'S IVORY THRONE

An earlier page was concerned with the ivory throne which King Solomon built for himself, a type of the triumphal aspect of the Incarnation. It recurs throughout a large part of Guerric's first Annunciation sermon, and gives him the occasion to speak of Mary's chastity:

> I would rather choose now to wonder at that ivory of virginal chastity, so precious, indeed so priceless. . . . How brilliant is that ivory which pleased the eyes of so great and so rich a king, in whose days silver was of no account; how cool — it did not even know the heat of passion in conception; how solid — even childbirth did not violate it; how white and at the same time how ruddy — it was filled by the whiteness of eternal light and the fire of Holy Spirit in all their fulness. . . . Mary found before the Lord a grace all her own, above that of all the elect, angels and men, the grace to conceive and bear God's Son and to have a throne of glory carved from the ivory of her body by the power of the most High without the labor of hands. . . . How blessed then is that womb of ivory from which the Redeemer's flesh of ivory was taken. . . . Happy indeed, my brethren, is the brilliance of that ivory, that is the whiteness of chasti-

46. Ser. 27, 2nd for Annunciation: 2; II, 40-41.

ty, before which our Solomon chooses neither the gold of worldly wisdom, the silver of eloquence nor the jewel of any favor. . . .[47]

The theme and the interpretation must have been fairly constant in Guerric's time. A few more lines will illustrate its development by Nicholas of Clairvaux:

> Of ivory, we are told. How is it that no account is taken[48] of gold, silver, precious stones, the splendor of all those materials which are more costly? The substance of ivory alone has so many qualities that something fashioned therein can be preferred to all else. For ivory has a wonderful lustre, is very strong, has the advantage too that it stays cool. Now was anything whiter than that virginity, so beautiful to look upon that it caught the eyes of all the host of heaven? What was stronger than the strength which was used by the Lord's own might to break in pieces the belongings of one who by nature was stronger? Did anything stay cooler than what was overshadowed by the power of the Most High, protected from the scorching of sin by the fulness of the Spirit coming from above? [49]

Returning to Guerric's Annunciation sermon — once more he states the condition without which Mary's chastity is of no avail — no more than that of the fallen angels. His next words are: " . . . provided that chastity is commended by humility, for the Lord 'has looked upon the humility of his handmaid'."[50]

He concludes the meditation by quoting a verse from the Song of Songs: "His belly [Hebrew: body] is ivory work, encrusted with sapphires."[51] He does not enlarge upon it, except to say that chastity must be adorned with other virtues; but it is worth noticing that there is something characteristic of Guerric here. He allows himself great freedom in

---

47. Ser. 26, 1st for Annunciation: 4-5; II, 35-36.

48. *Praetermittitur.* This reading seems evident. Migne has *praemittitur.*

49. Nicholas of Clairvaux, Sermon for Our Lady's Birthday; PL 144: 738-7; attributed to Saint Peter Damian.

50. Ser. 26, 1st for Annunciation: 5; II, 36.

51. Song 5:14.

applying to Mary texts which other commentators have reserved for her Son. Among these latter, with regard to this
particular verse, is the author who has continued Gregory's
commentary.[52] Rupert also has written a commentary which
from the outset is specifically Marian; but he has kept to his
own rules: this "belly of ivory" belongs to the Bridegroom,
not to the Bride, so it can be understood only of Christ.[53]
However, Guerric knows that he is allowing himself some
freedom here, and justifies it, he is not flinging texts around
irresponsibly. For the most part, he says, if we praise one we
praise the other, since the two are one flesh and one spirit.

The commentary on the ivory throne leads up to another
text from the Lamentations of Jeremiah, familiar to Guerric
in its liturgical form: "Whiter than snow, more ruddy than
old ivory."[54] He quotes it thus in the first place, but then
shews that he has in mind a similar verse from the Song of
Songs: "My beloved is white and ruddy." [55] The Gregorian
commentator (Robert) has understood this of Christ, white
by his innocence, red because he has washed us from our sins
in his blood.[56] Since this writer continued Gregory's commentary as late as the eleventh century, he was probably
following the Venerable Bede.[57] One should not be too solici-
tous in investigating sources for an interpretation which is so
obvious. But in fact the verse of Lamentations is so understood as far back as Origen. The white for him is purity; the
red is the martyrdom implied in an ascetic life.[58] Guerric
anyhow, according to the principle just given, refers it immediately to Mary:

> Mary herself is whiter than snow, more ruddy than old
> ivory; chastity gave her a whiteness beyond compare, and

52. Robert of Tombelaine, *On the Song of Songs*; PL 79:524BC. The commentary was and often is attributed to Saint Gregory the Great. See P. Verbraken,
Introd. to CCL 144, p. VIII-IX.
53. Rupert of Deutz, *On the Song of Songs*, 5; PL 168:926.
54. Lam 4:7; Responsory in Office of Apostles.
55. Song 5:10.
56. Robert, *On the Song*; PL 79:524BC.
57. Bede, *On the Song* 4:22; PL 91:1161CD.
58. Origen, *Selected commentaries on 'Lamentations'*; PG 13:653A.

charity, or indeed martyrdom, a ruddiness brighter than that of all the elect of old. For her own soul was pierced by a sword, so that the Mother of the Sovereign Virgin and Martyr might be a virgin and martyr herself. If her Beloved was "white and ruddy," so was she.[59]

So Mary is shown to us as a martyr. The Annunciation sermon sermon looks ahead already to the completed work of our Redemption.

### THE SCENT OF THIS FLOWER

Both at the Annunciation and on Our Lady's birthday we find the metaphor of sweet-smelling perfume. Christ says to his Bride: "The scent of your garments is like the scent of incense."[60] This is true even of us. If your prayer goes up to him as incense, he will be all the more often drawn to visit us. It seems even as though the privilege and the delight were his rather than ours. He will say as he comes to us: "I will hie me to the mountain of myrrh and the hill of frankincense."[61] But there is one of whom that has been supremely true. "Today he came to that highest mount of mountains, mount not only of myrrh and incense but also of all perfumes. I mean the Virgin of virgins, full of all graces. . . ." This perfume of graces — his own gifts, it is true — even drew the Lord into our world. Here is the end of the sermon: "This scent draws the Lord of majesty from on high and invites him to bend the heavens and come down. This is seen today when the Most High, after sending an angel from heaven, himself, too, comes down into his Mother's womb, he who is always in the Father's bosom, with whom he lives and reigns for ever and ever."[62]

Guerric had probably read the commentary on this verse which was available to him under the name of Saint Gregory the Great: "The Spouse goes to the mountain of myrrh and the hill of frankincense. He calls intimately upon those whom

59. Ser. 26, 1st for Annunciation: 4; II, 35.
60. Song 4:11.
61. Song 4:6.
62. Ser. 26, 1st for Annunciation: 6; II, 38.

he sees scaling the heights by mortification of their vices, those who reach him with the lovely scent of their pure and humble prayers."[63] Interpretations such as these show how closely the moral sense of Scripture — the soul's union with Christ the Spouse — is bound up in the minds of Guerric's predecessors and his own, with the allegorical — the Mystery of Christ himself.

The text here cited in Latin is *Ibo mihi* and not the usual *Vadam*: not simply, "I will go," but, as the Revised Standard Version has it: "I will hie me." The two Latin words, grammatically quite unjustifiable, suggest a nuance which it is difficult to translate into any modern language: "For myself I shall go" — "It will be my privilege and delight to go." Guerric has nothing to say about the *mihi*. After Bernard's death it fell to Gilbert of Hoyland to comment on this part of the inspired book. He found before him *Vadam mihi,* was struck by the second word in the sense suggested, and dwelt long upon it:

> Not only for him, but for myself will I go. . . . How sweet, how lovely it is, for me to go to her. It is for my own sake now that I will go. Such a journey is a profit and a delight to me; for my own sake then will I go. Even now the sweet fragrance of myrrh is blowing down from the mountain; it draws me on my way. For my sake will I go; it is my delight to stay with the Bride.[64]

63. Robert, *On the Song*; PL 79:510A.

64. Gilbert of Hoyland, *Sermon on the Song*, 28: 2; PL 184:146B. Incidentally the phrase *Ibo (Vadam) mihi,* gives us an interesting example of a patristic interpretation which is helped and inspired perhaps by a scribal error; certainly by an awkward and over-literal rendering, first from Hebrew into Greek, then from Greek into Latin.

I have consulted several patristic commentaries on the Song of Songs, but Gilbert's is the only one so far, besides Guerric's, in which I have found the second word *mihi.* The Vulgate has *Vadam* alone, and the critical revisors do not record any addition or variant in their threefold critical apparatus (*Biblia Sacra . . . ad codicum fidem*, vol. XI, Rome, 1957, p. 186). The librarian at Troyes tells me that ms. 458 (known as the Bible of Saint Bernard: see Introduction in SCh 166:77) reads only *Vadam.* The Igny Bible, ms. 72, does not go as far as the Song of Songs.

Although not competent to discuss the Hebrew, I am told that the construction *'elech li* is quite regular, and have been referred to Gen 12:1; 22:2; to several places in the Song 2:10 (twice); 2:11; 2:13. Literally it means "I will go to me,"

The first sermon for Our Lady's birthday is a commentary on a text which is expressed in the same metaphor: "Like a vine I bore sweet-smelling fruit."[65] Guerric is aware that the words are spoken of Wisdom, that is of Christ, but he invokes a rule of Scripture, according to which many things said of Christ can be said of his Mother also. If she was the flower, then Christ was the perfume. Not only are we drawn to the sweet-smelling Christ, whom he offers to us; but God the Father, delighted with that odor, looks all the more kindly on us, whose nature his Son has taken: "Behold, the smell of my son is as the smell of a field which the Lord has blessed."[66]

Once again, Guerric is only developing a metaphor which is traditional. Saint Ambrose has already recognized in Christ the scent and fruit of this vine, and has applied it to Isaac's blessing.[67] Saint Augustine has returned to it several times, usually with reference to the words of Isaac. "For the Lord was first, to those who believe unto life, a good odor; a bad odor to those who persecute to the death. "[68] "Behold, the smell of my son. . . . Isaac smelt the clothing and said that it was the smell of a field. In the heart of this mystery see Christ; in the clothing see Christ's Church."[69] "Behold, the smell of my son. . . . Like a field, the world is filled with the odor of Christ's name."[70]

Mary is a flower, Christ the perfume. Or even before the Incarnation, the Son of God was drawn by the sweet odor of her graces. Our own human nature in Christ is sweet to the

---

and should be rendered "I will betake myself." I have found only one English translation which takes account of it in Song 4:6: the Revised Standard Version as quoted above. As for the awkward interruption of the passage in the second person — I am told that in the old Hebrew script an *aleph* may easily have been written by mistake for a *tau*. If in fact this happened, the original was *telech li*: "you will betake yourself."

65. Sir 24:23 according to Vulgate; cf. RSV 24:17. Ser. 51, first for Our Lady's Birthday; II, 192ff.

66. Gen 27:27.

67. Ambrose, *The Days of Creation*, 3:72; PL 14:187A.

68. Augustine, *Sermon on the Old Testament*, 4:38; CCL 41:40-41.

69. *Ibid.*, 4:24; CCL 41:38.

70. Augustine, *City of God*, 16:37; Everyman's Library, vol. 2, p. 136 (Dutton: N.Y., 1947).

Father, so that he looks all the more kindly to us: we ourselves are now the field which the Lord has blessed. The
sweet scent of Isaac's son is Christ and is also his clothing, the
Church. The whole world is different from what it was before
Christ's coming: it is a field where now the Father and we
ourselves, too, can smell the sweet odor of Christ. But what is
the flower which smells so sweetly that the world is different
from what it ever was before? It is Mary, endowed with such
graces that even God has been drawn to her.

Mary, by God's invitation and her own free choice, became
the Mother of God and the Mother of our Redemption. This
can give rise to much speculation and to many distinctions;
but this is not the place for them. Our mediaeval writers for
the most part were content with types and symbols; these
perhaps brought them as near as could be to the heart of the
Mystery. Their imagery becomes richer than it does in any
other field, when they speak of a humble and chaste Virgin,
who was overshadowed by the Holy Spirit and became the
Mother of God. The few interpretations of Scripture recorded here may show that Guerric was simply speaking a language which he had learned from Fathers of the Church who
wrote before him. Amedeus of Lausanne devoted his homilies
to Mary from beginning to end,[71] otherwise it is difficult to
find an author who is so ready as Guerric to speak of her. She
always takes her place in the Mystery of God's salvation offered to us through Jesus Christ, so that it has not been easy
to devote pages to his Marian teaching in particular; impossible certainly to separate Mary from the Mystery of Christ.
Bernard has been called the *citharista Mariae,* and the slogan
*de Maria numquam satis* has been quoted to us as his: "Of
Mary we can never say enough." However, in proportion to
the corpus of each one's writings, Guerric has far more to
say. This study should help a reader to judge whether he may
be more original,[72] and whether he is hardly less eloquent
must be a matter for each one's taste.

71. Amedeus of Lausanne, *Homilies on the Blessed Virgin Mary;* SCh 72, CF 18.
72. Cf. Introduction; CF 8, pp. xxxiv-xxxviii.

CHAPTER EIGHT

# CHRIST'S KNOWLEDGE AND BLISS SHARED WITH US

## CHRIST'S KNOWLEDGE OUR OWN

"WHILE DEEP SILENCE ENVELOPED ALL things, and night in its swift course was now half gone, your all-powerful Word, O Lord, came from the royal throne."[1]

This is the thought which inspires much of Guerric's fifth Christmas sermon. Christ has come down in silence; is found silent in the manger. Yet, by a supreme title, he is Word and Wisdom. A dominating theme here is that our knowledge is bound up with Christ's, a sharing of his. It seems realistic, certainly more in accord with our author's mind, to treat of the two together; provided that we avoid confusion by making distinctions when necessary.

Nothing could better commend to us the value of silence than the Word of God, silent among men. Such he is; yet he is the Word by whom all things were made. But that Word of God himself learned in the schooling of his Mother. We would prefer to remain silent, so that, just as Christ learned from his Mother, so we may learn the profound secrets which lie hid in that divine silence:

If I were allowed, I would gladly be dumb and brought low, and be silent even from good things, that I might be able the more attentively and diligently to apply my ear to the secret utterances and sacred meanings of this divine silence, learning in silence in the school of the Word, if only for so

1. Wis 18:14-15, in liturgical form. Antiphon within Octave of Christmas.

79

long as the Word himself was silent under the schooling of
his Mother."²

Christ learned from a human Mother; but what a store of
Wisdom is at our disposal, if we will be silent and learn from
him. Christ's knowledge: then ours. The "school (*schola*) of
the Word" in which we learn is balanced against the "schooling (*disciplina*) of his Mother" which is the school for him. In
the very sentence which speaks of our "learning," there is
mention also of "divine silence" in which there are "sacred
utterances and sacred meanings." For the moment it seems
better to abstain from distinctions between divine, human
and acquired knowledge, and to present Guerric's texts as
they are.

When we have said "the Word," we have said most that can
be said of the One who is with us in silence. Until the time of
the Council of Nicaea the first verses of Saint John's Prologue
were universally punctuated and read as follows: " . . . the
Word was God . . . all things were made through him . . .
what was made of life in him."³ All things, which at any time
should be, had life — *were* life — in the mind of God which
was the Word. The same punctuation was the more common
throughout the Middle Ages, and has remained in the Cistercian liturgy to this day. This Word, this knowledge of all
things, is here silent in our midst. The writers of the Middle
Ages gave expression to this by using a text of Isaiah. The
Vulgate text, literally translated, reads: "The Lord God of
hosts will make a consummation and a shortening in the
midst of all the land."⁴ A literal translation from the Septuagint — *logon syntetmêmenon* — gave the Latin *Verbum
abbreviatum,* and writers were not slow to take advantage of
this. What a mystery: that God should have "shortened,"
given us within limits, the Word who is Infinite. Guerric then
encourages us to learn from Christ: "It is a shortened word,

2. Ser. 10, 5th for Christmas: 2; I, 63-64.
3. Jn 1:1-4. The Jerusalem Bible has returned to the old punctuation, as given above.
4. Is 10, 23. The Hebrew is simply emphasizing the idea of 'end' or 'destruction'.

yet in such a way that in it every word which makes for salvation is summed up. "[5]

The theme is pursued. We have now, on the level of knowledge, what we have contemplated already on the level of being. If the Infinite God has been conceived in a Virgin's womb, we can better understand that he has put his infinite knowledge within our range. Once again, we cannot reflect upon the knowledge given to us except as a sharing of Christ's. "But is it surprising that the Word should have shortened all his words to us, when he willed to be shortened himself and in some way lessened, so much that he straitened himself from his incomprehensible immensity to the confines of a womb, and he who contains the world suffered himself to be contained in a manger?" In heaven the Word — and the Word means knowledge — overcomes the most exalted of those creatures whom God has endowed with understanding. At Bethlehem he is handled and is the food of the very simplest of men. This idea of food will have a large place in Guerric's later development. "In heaven this Word is so high and dreaded that the angelic powers are overcome with awe; in the manger he feeds the simple and the stupid. There the keenest understanding of an angel cannot search him; here he can be touched even by the dull senses of men."[6] In that manger, if anywhere, he hides his wisdom from the wise and prudent and reveals it to little ones. Yet again we hear of the Word (knowledge) which is shortened, brought within our limited range: " . . . let us make our way to Bethlehem . . . that in this visible and shortened Word we may learn the Wisdom of God, which in its entirety has been made humility."[7] Christ, infinite knowledge, is the Word; also he is Wisdom. But what of that Wisdom in this passing life — *interim*? (Both Bernard and Guerric constantly choose this word *interim* for our time of waiting, which is passing away.[8]) It

5. Ser. 10, 5th for Christmas: 3; I, 64.
6. *Ibid.*
7. *Ibid.*: 4; I, 65,
8. E.g. three times in Guerric's Ser. 6, 1st for Christmas: 2, 3, 4; I, 40, 42: "He prefers to present himself as a Child . . . that *for this while* he may excite rather our love." "If he is in truth powerful and terrible, yet *for this while* he hides it

seems that the Eternal Wisdom now wishes to know nothing except that humility, the self-humiliation of the Virgin's womb and of Bethlehem; so that Wisdom may be able to teach simply this: " . . . that supreme Wisdom has willed *for this present while* to know nothing else but that humility of which he willed afterwards to declare himself a teacher."[9]

If we are learning, Christ is learning all the time, too. He is not ignorant of the meaning of humility. If we would wish to distinguish between divine and human knowledge, yet we find them strangely combined in a few words. He knows what humility is by virtue of the Nature which he receives from the Father: he draws this knowledge also from his Mother: "Although he knew it well, by origin from his mother and naturally from his Father, yet even from his mother's womb he learned it from the things he suffered."[10]

Again, all that is undertaken for the moment is to record Guerric's phrases, without immediately placing them in categories and drawing distinctions. Yet, if Christ is God and Man, he knows both as God and as Man. Divine and human knowledge in Christ: we have no need to wait for scholastic refinements to teach us this. In the last place we have found them recognized in a striking contrast. He has knowledge which is first "natural from his Father," then "by origin from his Mother"; something which belongs to his divine Nature and also something which the Child has drawn from his Mother. In nearly every context, Christ's knowledge, divine or human, has been the exemplar or the source of our own.

### THE SCHOOL OF PHILOSOPHY

In the above context Guerric has used these words of ourselves and of Christ. This seems the best place to make some observations on the use of the word *schola*, since it implies that Christ is our Teacher. Elsewhere it is joined to the idea

---

all." "Sweet it is *for this present while* to think and think over again of God as a Child." Bernard, *Apologia to Abbot William:* 17; CF 1:54: "The soul is indeed bereaved of its heavenly bridegroom *for this present while.*"

9. Ser. 10, 5th for Christmas: 4; I, 65. Another example of *interim*.
10. *Ibid.*
11. Ser. 10, 5th for Christmas: 2, I, 63-64.

of Christian philosophy. The two are akin and had best be
treated together. Christ is the supreme Master and Philosopher. Quite obviously — and throughout all the treatment of
knowledge — the science imparted in this school is far more
than a grasp of concepts.

Since Christ is both teaching and learning, and we are learning all the time, we find ourselves in a school. *Schola* most
especially is a word common in that monastic tradition in
which Guerric has been brought up. It appears, coupled again
with *disciplina*, in the first sermon for the feast of Saint
Benedict: "Blessed are you also, my brethren, who have en-
rolled in the study (*disciplina*) of wisdom, the school (*schola*)
of Christian philosophy."[12] The legislator for monks himself
proposed to found a "school of the Lord's service."[13]

We have seen already how it is a matter of principle for
Guerric that what is said of Christ, can be said also, due
measure being observed, of his Mother. Those two words —
*schola* and *disciplina* — have been found together in a place
which must have been familiar to Guerric, where Mary is put
before us as a model of one who learns. The author, probably
Paschasius, speaks of her with the Apostles in the Upper
Room, awaiting the descent of the Comforter at Pentecost:
"The Virgin spends her time with the apostles in the *school*
where virtue is being taught . . . that we may find in her the
form and example of Christ's *schooling*."[14]

Guerric's use of *schola,* as quoted above from his fifth
Christmas sermon, may be put beside two others from Saint
Bernard. The three together bring into relief the part of
Christ: "School of the Word,"[15] "School of Christ,"[16]
"School of the Savior."[17] Then what is it that Christ teaches
us? This appears from the other uses of *schola*: "School of
virtues" and "School of humility."[18] This last phrase was

12. Ser. 22, 1st for St Benedict: 4; II, 5.

13. Rule of St Benedict, Prologue.

14. Paschasius Radbertus, *Letter to Paula and Eustochium,* known under the
name of Jerome: 4; PL 30:125D.

15. *Loc. cit.*

16. Bernard, *Sermon on St John Baptist*: 1; OB 5:176; CF 25.

17. Bernard, Sermons *De diversis* 22:2, 5; 30:1; OB 6-1:171, 173, 214.

18. Bernard, *Degrees of Humility* 21; *Praises of the Virgin Mother* 4:10; OB
3:32; 4:55; CF 13 and 43.

found also in a text of another little-known Cistercian, Hugh of Barzelle.[19] One virtue is supreme. Etienne Gilson recognized that the teaching of the Cistercians was directed to this virtue when he wrote his book on Saint Bernard's mystical theology and entitled one chapter: "The School of Charity."[20] I have not found the phrase textually in Saint Bernard, but William of Saint Thierry tells his monks that they have inscribed themselves as specialists in this school. Its aim is real knowledge, but knowledge which comes from the very truth of things and from a man's experience; not merely from subtlety in argument:

> This is the school which specializes in charity. Here it is studied and ardently discussed. At the conclusion of a disputation the answer is found not so much by argument; rather by reason itself, by realism and experience.[21]

Our progress in knowledge and love comes from the Blessed Trinity. Christ promised to send a Comforter; so the "School of Christ" is also the "School of the Spirit." Bernard acknowledges this on the feast of Pentecost: "I rejoice that you are students in this school, the school of the Spirit. Here you are schooled in goodness, discipline and knowledge, so that you may say with the sacred writer: 'I had more understanding than all my teachers'."[22]

To belong to this school is a privilege, but it is not merely a privilege and a luxury. As laborious as the life of a student anywhere, it has all those ups and downs which consist of graces and consolations, then the temptation to throw all aside and give up: "The one who makes progress in this school of virtue must suffer many a change. Now it is the visit of grace, now the testing of temptation, the one that he may not faint on the way, the other that he may not swell with pride."[23]

19. Hugh of Barzelle, *On brethren living together*; ed. J. Morson, *Studia anselmiana* 41 (1957), 127.

20. Etienne Gilson, *The Mystical Theology of Saint Bernard* (Westminster, 1940), ch 3: *Schola caritatis*, pp. 60 ff.

21. William of Saint Thierry, *The Nature and Dignity of Love* 26; CF 15.

22. Bernard, *Sermon for Pentecost* 3:5; OB 5:173; CF 22.

23. Bernard, Sermon *De diversis* 3:1; OB 6-1:86-87; CF 40:1; OB 6-1:235.

This has been said by occasion of the word *schola*. I have found it only twice in the writings of Guerric; yet it sums up a tradition for him. He will have read at some time the other texts here quoted: almost certainly those of Saint Bernard, probably the others also.

The other word which he uses — "Philosophy" — has a long Christian tradition behind it. " . . . you have inscribed your names for the study (*disciplina*) of wisdom and for the school of Christian philosophy."[24] Origen uses the word several times when he is speaking of the stages of the spiritual life in the Prologue to his Commentary on the Song of Songs.[25] The work *De Instituto Christiano* is written especially for monks; but they are never called monks, always philosophers. (The authorship and history of this work have been discussed interminably; but I regard it as a writing of Saint Gregory of Nyssa).[26] When early Christians used this word "philosopher," evidently they meant to baptize a pagan word and idea. Saint Cyprian shows that he means by it something new, to be contrasted with what it had been for the pagans: "But we, dear brothers, are philosophers not in word but in deed. It is not by dressing in a gown that we profess wisdom, by by embracing the truth."[27]

The word is often used by Saint Bernard in a pejorative sense,[28] but not always. He will use it of the Christian or monastic way of life in contrast to the worldly. Here are the two in a few words: " . . . how does Paul's philosophy excel the philosophy of the wise of this world."[29] He has a passage

24. Ser. 22, 1st for St Benedict: 4; II, 5.

25. Origen, *Commentary on the Song of Songs, Prologue: Ancient Christian Writers* 26, pp. 43, 44, 45.

26. Gregory of Nyssa, *De Instituto Christiano (Christian Formation)*. Migne is useless here; it is essential to read the work in Werner Jaeger's critical edition: *Gregorii Nysseni Opera* VIII/1. See the discussion by Louis Bouyer, in *The Spirituality of the New Testament and the Fathers* (English edition, 1960), pp. 358 ff., 370 ff.

27. Cyprian, *De bono patientiae (The goodness of Patience)*: 3; PL 4:647. Cf Du Cange, *Glossarium mediae et infimae latinitatis*, a small article *Philosophia*, where the first entry is from Isidore of Pelusium, *Vita monastica* I, 260. Much more ample information is found in G. W. H. Lampe's *Patristic Greek Lexicon* (Oxford, 1961).

28. Bernard, *De diversis* 7:2; OB 6-1:108; CF 46.

29. *Ibid.* 1.

which does not in fact contain the word *philosophia,* but possibly surpasses the one just quoted from Saint Cyprian: "What did the holy apostles teach, and what do they teach us now? Fishing, landscape gardening or anything of the kind? How to read Plato, or untie the knots of Aristotle; always to be learning and never getting as far as the knowledge of the truth? No: they have taught me how to live."[30] Bernard tells us here that the aim of true learning is knowledge, knowledge of the truth and of the truth by which we live.

There is no need to dwell any longer upon the word *philosophia*; in fact Dom Jean Leclercq has devoted a whole chapter to it in one of his publications.[31] It has claimed our attention because Guerric has linked it up with Christ's *schola* and *disciplina.* The section which is being written now is concerned with Christ's knowledge and our sharing it. Guerric has one more place in which he says that Christ crucified is himself the supreme philosophy: "Let Paul then speak . . . of Christ crucified, who is to those who court their own ruin foolishness, but to me and those who are on the road to salvation truly God's power and God's wisdom. For me this is the loftiest and most noble philosophy."[32]

Christ knows from all eternity. His Being and his Knowledge are born of the Father. Whatever truth he teaches us above the level of our unaided reason is a communication of what the Father has given him. This very same Christ, an infant in the manger and a Child in the home at Nazareth, learns from his Mother. Here he is the model for those who belong to his *schola,* his *disciplina.* Mary in her turn is our example when she waits for the Spirit. Whatever knowledge in any way we receive from Christ, is for our true life; more than any other knowledge it deserves the name "philosophy."

30. Bernard, *SS. Peter and Paul* 1:3; OB 5:189-190; CF 25.
31. Jean Leclercq, *Etudes sur le vocabulaire du Moyen-Age; Studia anselmiana* 48, ch. 2, p. 39-67. See also *The Love of Learning and the Desire for God* (New York: Fordham, 1961), pp. 127-129.
32. Ser. 30, 2nd for Palm Sunday: 1; II, 59.

### EATING WITH CHRIST IN THE GATE BEFORE THE LORD

The third Annunciation sermon takes up the theme of divine knowledge, knowledge which we are meant to share. It proceeds on lines very similar to those of the last Christmas sermon, which has already provided matter for our meditation. Guerric has spoken of the utter self-humiliation of the Word made Flesh in Mary's womb. The Eternal Word is subdued in silence. Yet this is a silence which cries out to us: "It is to you, brethren, to you, that the Word's silence is speaking, is crying out, commending to you the discipline of silence."[33] Again this silence is not negative; something must fill it. This time it is not so laborious; we are to spend the silence in eating our bread, following the example of Christ himself. Once more we meet the triumphal aspect of the Incarnation: Solomon's ivory throne. In the first Annunciation sermon it was the body taken by the Word; this time it is Mary's womb in which he is conceived. Here the Prince sits to eat his bread; more than this, he invites us to come and sup with him.

Ezekiel saw the eastern gate of the sanctuary closed. No man could pass through it, for the Lord God of Israel had gone that way; it would remain closed for the Prince. He, the Prince, would sit in that gate and eat his bread before the Lord. "This gate shall remain shut; it shall not be opened, and no one shall enter by it; for the Lord, the God of Israel has entered by it; therefore it shall remain shut. Only the Prince may sit in it to eat breat before the Lord."[34]

There is bread at this supper. The great mystery is that the one who eats and the Bread which is eaten are one and the same. Christ feeds on no other Bread than himself. The Word by its very nature is that Bread. The Flesh — that is the Humanity — is that Bread because of its union with the Word. "The Word feeds upon the Word; the Son lives upon himself, for as the Father has life in himself, so he has given

---

33. Ser. 28, 3rd for Annunciation: 5; II, 52.
34. Ezek 44:2-3. Guerric, *ibid.*

to the Son to have life in himself."[35] We have read a few lines above that we are invited to go in and sup with him. Almost in the same breath as what has just been quoted, we hear of the word coming from the mouth of God which gives life to man: "Neither does man live by bread alone, but by every word which comes forth from the mouth of God."[36] The author is so bold as to say that this word does not merely come from, but itself is the One and Only-Begotten Word of the Father. He explains this a little further: the Only-Begotten Word is simple without distinctions; yet he contains within himself the concept and the form of any word which God may speak.

As we read on, we learn that there is something else besides. "In another way, but yet with unspeakable beatitude and incomparable happiness, that Prince, sitting in the gate of the virginal womb, ate the bread of the Word before the Lord."[37] Guerric may be left to comment upon this himself. Whatever the meaning of the sentence, once again we are to do what Christ does. "That will be the occupation, if you are wise, which will keep you busy in your silence: to eat the bread of God's Word before the Lord, preserving like Mary what is said about Christ and pondering it in your heart." Surely it will be our privilege and delight to eat the Bread of the Word before the Lord, just as he does, following the example of Mary. But we hear immediately that Christ himself will be privileged and delighted. If he is our food, we shall be his food also. "Christ will take pleasure in eating this bread with you, and he who feeds you will himself be fed in you ... " For us this Bread will never fail, " ... and the more the bread itself is eaten the more it will abound ... since grace is not lessened by use but increased."

There is never any doubt, of course, that Christ, God and Man, has knowledge both divine and human. Guerric does not confuse them; but it is sometimes difficult to say that he is speaking of one or the other. All the better: he is so fully

35. Jn 5:26. Ser. 28, 3rd for Annunciation: 6; II, 53.
36. Deut 8:3. Mt 4:4.
37. *Ibid.*; but the text quoted is that of the earlier manuscripts.

conscious that it is one Person who knows. Much less are we justified in trying to apply precise distinctions to what he says of Christ as Man. We shall return to this place; but one thing is very clear. What is said of Christ is immediately applied to us. De Lubac was struck with this passage (even though he had a faulty text before him), and thought it a remarkable illustration of his thesis: that allegorical exegesis and moral or mystical interpretation were not separate, hardly distinct: one was contained in the other.[38] "In that gate then the Prince sat and ate bread, for 'if anyone,' he says, 'will open to me, I will come in to him and sup with him and he with me'." "That Prince, sitting in the gate of the virginal womb, ate the bread of the Word before the Lord."[39]

### GUERRIC IN RELATION TO SOME MODERN THEOLOGIANS

This may be the best place in which to consider the teaching of a few modern writers concerning Christ, his knowledge, and his relation to us as source and exemplar. They may give us points of comparison or contrast with Guerric speaking from the twelfth century.

A confrère once asked me to reflect upon the teaching of Jean-Jacques Olier.

"In the holy mystery of the Incarnation the sacred humanity of Our Lord was brought to nothing in its own person, in such a way that it no longer sought itself, had no interest of its own, acted for itself no longer. It had in itself another person substituted, that of the Son of God. . . ."[40] Here is our model. The sacred humanity is made to speak to us in these words: "Just as my Father, when he sent me, cut off every root of self-seeking, in not giving me the human person; but united me to a divine Person that I might live for him; so you . . . ."

Now who is this "I," so detached from all that he has not

---

38. De Lubac, *Exégèse mediévale*, 1:599 and n. 3.
39. Ser. 28, 3rd for Annunciation: 5, 6; II, 53.
40. J. J. Olier, *Catéchisme de la Vie Intérieure*, leçon 20, col 477-9. The translation is a very literal one from Olier's French. The passage is quoted by Emile Mersch in *The Whole Christ* (Bruce: Milwaukee, 1938), p. 551.

received a human personality, telling us that God has united him to a divine Person? Can the human nature of Christ stand aside and speak like this? What is most surprising is the idea of the humanity of Christ "brought to nothing in its own person" ( . . . *anéantie en sa propre personne*). In what person? It had "another person substituted"; but "other" makes no sense unless there are two terms of reference. Mersch does not critize Olier (see note 40), he cites him as a master; but he writes a note here to say that Olier must be "explained." otherwise his teaching would be Monothelist. Would it be rather Nestorian? Could it be countenanced by Pope Leo the Great: "So the Son of God enters the weakness of our world . . .The impassible God did not disdain to become a man subject to suffering. . . . For he who is truly God is also truly man."[41]

This is not criticism for its own sake. Olier's purpose is to put the Mystery of the Incarnation before us as a model for our sanctification; that is also the purpose of Mersch in quoting him. Perhaps the contrast may help us appreciate a Guerric of Igny nurtured on the Fathers of the Church. He has spoken to us of the Prince eating his Bread in the Gate, the Word living on the Word, the Son on himself. This is not followed by an artificial moral application. The Word living on the Word in Eternity has become the Prince eating his bread in the gate, only that we may eat with him.

No claim is made here to an over-all evaluation of Olier. The query is raised only with regard to this christological passage, the more familiar because Mersch has transcribed it at length. Of Columba Marmion it is possible to speak with more confidence and in more general terms. "It may be said that the human nature in Jesus is stripped of its entire self, without attachment to any creature: *relictis omnibus.* . . . Having nothing of its own, not belonging to itself, it clings to the Word with all its might." A little later Marmion quotes

Bossuet: "Man[42] is raised up ... in Jesus Christ. Man is entirely under the guidance of the Word, who takes Man to himself. Man thus raised up and guided has no thought, no inner movement which is not divine."[43] Bossuet continues to develop this last sentence. If it were understood strictly, it would be difficult to see how it could be anything but a combination of Apollinarism and Monothelitism; but no doubt Bossuet's reader should make some allowance for rhetorical hyperbole. Obviously these authors acknowledge expressly the union of two natures in one Person. In this context it has been impossible to give more than isolated sentences; which cannot do them full justice.[44] Of Bossuet I am not competent to speak in general terms. Marmion has been the occasion of a renewed spiritual life and outlook for many. He was a pioneer of the "rapprochement" between theology and spirituality, so long divorced. But it is a mistake to use the formulations of Councils or of scholastic theologians and then to make purely artificial applications of these to our spiritual lives. Once again, we are far from Chalcedon: " ... The Son of God ... invisible in his own, he became visible in ours; the incomprehensible wished to be comprehended."[45] The relevance to ourselves is there already.

We may go back before Chalcedon to Saint Cyril of Alexandria, the supreme example — not of "interiorization," but rather of a dogmatic exposition which does not need to be "interiorized," because from the beginning it bears upon our life of union with God. The intention of the writers just quoted is doubtless the same; but their ideas and their language are not those of the most ancient tradition. "Consub-

42. I am responsible for the translation from French. The translator of the English edition did in fact render "L'homme" literally: "The man." Marmion (or his editor) seems to have been a little perplexed here, for he thought it necessary to insert "la nature humaine" in square brackets.

43. "En Jésus-Christ l'homme, absolument soumis à la direction du Verbe, qui l'élève à soi, n'a que des pensées et des mouvements divins."

44. Columba Marmion, *Sponsa Verbi,* (English ed. 1925), p. 26-29. Bossuet, *Discours sur l'histoire universelle,* 2ᵉ partie, ch. 19: *Jésus-Christ et sa doctrine.*

45. DS 294; TCC 250.

stantial with God, Christ is consubstantial with men by his human birth. Emmanuel, God with us and one of us, he becomes united to us physically by taking our flesh. Between him and us there is a solidarity real and efficacious."[46] "Of necessity then the one who supremely exists has been born in the flesh, and has taken everything of ours to himself, that the offspring of the flesh, that is we ourselves, on the way as we were to be corrupted and destroyed, may now abide in him. What was ours he has for his own, that we may have what was his." These last words are taken from a work by Cyril which bears the title: *That Christ is One.*[47] But this oneness of Christ is the chief preoccupation of Guerric of Igny; or rather it is what he always presupposes. Who is nearer to the old tradition: those authors who speak of the humanity of Christ no longer seeking itself but clinging to the Word; or Guerric, for whom that one Prince is sitting in the gate, eating his Bread before the Lord, and inviting us to go in and sup with him?

In an outstanding essay, *Current Problems in Christology*, Karl Rahner suggests the possibility of passing from an ontic (*ontische*) Christology to an existential one, by which he means statements about Christ's spiritual relationship to the Father, which would be relevant to our own spiritual lives. He may have in mind the efforts made in this direction by Olier, Bossuet, and Marmion. The following passage is quoted from the translation by Cornelius Ernst, which is reliable in the sense that is is extremely literal. "Suppose someone says: 'Jesus is the man whose life is one of absolutely unique self-surrender to God.' He may very well have stated the truth about the very depths of what Christ really is, *provided* that he has understood (a) that this self-abandonment presupposes a communication of God to the man; (b) that an absolute self-surrender implies an absolute communication of God to the man, one which makes what is produced by it into the reality of the producer himself."[48]

46. Hubert du Manoir de Juaye, *Dogme et Spiritualité chez Saint Cyrille d'Alexandrie* (1944), pp. 172-173.

47. Cyril of Alexandria, *Quod unus sit Christus*; PG 75:1268C.

48. Karl Rahner *Theological Investigations* I, pp. 149-200: *Current Problems in Christology*. Our passage is on p. 172.

Now from this way of speaking it is difficult not to receive the impression that there is already in existence a man to whom God can make this communication of himself. We are concerned with the hypostatic union, and there is no Man Jesus until our human nature has already been assumed. Has Ernst led us astray in translating *den Menschen* (twice) as "the man"? Or could Rahner's words have been better chosen? Would he have done better to say "human nature," "humanity" ; (*Menschlieit*), or simply "Man" (*Menschk*) without the define article?

What is most to the purpose, is to observe that in Guerric of Igny — and in how many of the Fathers — there is no need for any distinction between an "ontic" and an "existential" Christology. Whatever God has revealed, whatever the Church has taught, has already relevance to our spiritual life. The allegorical sense of Scripture is already moral and spiritual. "What is a mystery for your redemption is also an example for your imitation . . . if you will faithfully receive the Word from the mouth of the heavenly messenger you, too, may conceive the God whom the whole world cannot contain, conceive him however in your heart, not in your body. And yet even in your body . . . since the Apostle bids us glorify and bear God in our body."[49] De Lubac is inspired by Guerric and others to speak of an *intériorisation*, a moral and spiritual sense, which is necessarily contained in Scripture when it speaks of the Incarnation and Redemption.[50] The Father gives it to the Son to have life in himself; we are raised up to share this same life. If we are seeking a remedy for somewhat artificial — hardly orthodox — applications of doctrine, can we do better than return to the Fathers of the Church or to the Middle Ages?

The past three decades have witnessed a prolonged and intricate discussion concerning Christ's psychological activity. Any assessment of the knowledge of Christ must be in accord with the defined truth of two natures in one Person. All who have accepted and understood the dogma of Chalcedon have acknowledged both divine and human knowledge in the

49. Ser. 27, 2nd for Annunciation: 4; II, 44-45.
50. H. De Lubac, *Exégèse mediévale* 1:555 and n. 3.

single One who knows. Human nature, of itself finite, is a
mystery which has posed many problems. We have long been
familiar with the distinction made by Saint Thomas: the man
Christ enjoys the beatific vision; besides this he has knowledge infused and also acquired as men usually acquire it.[51]
The controversy and the definition at Chalcedon were on the
ontological level. From this arises the discussion of Christ's
psychology. To say nothing of what has been quoted from
Guerric of Igny — the place just cited from Saint Thomas
shows that the question is not a new one: indeed it has been
prominent since the seventh century, when the Church was
faced with the Monothelite heresy. An important and intricate part of this general question is the particular one: how
was Christ humanly conscious of his divinity during his earthly life? Throughout the last century, and in the earlier part
of this, any attempt to probe the problem was likely to incur
the suspicion of Rationalism or Modernism: hence the condemnation of several propositions attributed to Modernists in
the decree *Lamentabili* of 1907, and in another issued from
the Holy Office more than ten years later.[52] Twenty years
were to pass before Paul Galtier made his penetrating study
of Christ's psychology.[53] Unable to conceive how Christ in
his human nature can be directly aware of his union with the
god-head, Galtier finds the answer in the beatific vision accorded to Christ in his earthly life — as he says, according to
the teaching of all theologians.[54] The second world war pre-
vented any immediate reaction to Galtier's work and gave the
theologians time to reflect. Another land-mark came in 1958:
Bernard Lonergan's *De constitutione Christi ontologica et
psychologica*. Christ knows that he is God by virtue of a
consciousness, a self-consciousness, analogous to that which
is presupposed by the activity of any rational being. Since
this is not a mere human self-consciousness, but a direct
knowledge of the godhead to which the human nature is

51. Thomas Aquinas, *Summa Theol.* 1, 3, 9-12.
52. DS 3432-3435, 3645-3647. TCC 304-307, 311-313.
53. Paul Galtier, *L'unité du Christ Etre-Personne-Conscience* (1939).
54. p. 358.

hypostatically united, it is in fact the beatific vision.[55] But Jean Galot questions this.[56] It has always been difficult for theologians, perhaps still more difficult for simple believers, to be entirely convinced that if Christ is *in termino,* he is one of themselves, like them in all things save sin; difficult also to reconcile consummated and final bliss with interior suffering and dereliction. Even without the beatific vision, says Galot, Christ knows that he is God simply because he is aware of himself. Before Lonergan and Galot, Karl Rahner had already written the first of two articles, already quoted. Both were printed later in his *Schriften zur Theologie* (rather roughly corresponding to the English *Theological Investigations*).[57] There is a direct, indeed an immediate, vision of the godhead; but the declarations of the Church's magisterium do not oblige us to hold that this is Christ's final beatitude. He is basically and subjectively aware of himself as Son of God. Here is the direct vision which is bound up with the union of the two natures, not something accorded to the human nature as a favor.

The paragraph just written is a very brief sketch of a prolonged and difficult theological debate. It is Guerric of Igny who concerns us, and we have before us one of those passages which is at the summit of his theological reflection. It would be useful, if possible, to clarify his relation to our contemporaries; though not in a tendentious way, not as being over-anxious to suggest that he anticipated the solution of any contemporary theologian.

" 'The Prince himself shall sit in the gate, to eat bread before the Lord.' . . . This supper is not without bread, since he who sups in the Bread of Life, the bread 'which today comes down from heaven and gives life to the world.' But it

55. Bernard Lonergan, *De constitutione Christi ontologica et psychologica* (1958).

56. Jean Galot, *Science et conscience de Jésus; Nouvelle Revue Théologique* 8 (2), (1960), 113-121.

57. Karl Rahner, *Schriften zur Theologie*: I, *Probleme der Christologie von heute,* p. 169-222. II, *Dogmatische Erwägungen über das Weissen und Selbstbewusstsein Christi,* p. 222-245; to which correspond *Theological Investigations:* I, *Current Problems in Christology,* p. 149-200 (see p. 168-173). V, *Dogmatic Reflections on the Knowledge and Self-Consciousness of Christ,* p. 193-215.

is a matter for wonder if he who eats and that which is eaten are one and the same, and he who eats is himself the bread which is eaten by him. Truly a matter for wonder, but it is very truth, for Christ does not feed on any bread other than himself."[58]

Christ eats his bread before the Lord. The one who eats and the bread which is eaten are the same. Now if this is concerned with divine knowledge alone, it has no bearing upon our discussion. But here are Guerric's words immediately following: "For he is wholly bread: the Word on his own account, the flesh on account of its union with the Word." True enough: this is put before us as the object of knowledge. However, is not the one who knows the Word Incarnate, deriving nourishment from himself, the Bread of Life? We ourselves are always careful to make it clear whether we are speaking of Christ's divine or human knowledge. We may even be cautious to excess, and in danger of separating the two knowledges in a Nestorian sense. There is a danger always of our projecting our mentality into a pre-scholastic author. Although Guerric knows that the one knowledge is not the other, he is far more fully conscious of and preoccupied with the one Christ who knows; immediately conscious also that this is a knowledge which Christ has come to share with us.

If the author's thought has been followed aright — admittedly the exegesis is obscure — this is strangely reminiscent of what modern theologians have been calling the basic and subjective awareness which Christ has of himself in the hypostatic union. Beatific knowledge has been set aside, because of a sentence which must next be considered.

HAS CHRIST THE KNOWLEDGE OF THE BLESSED?

The question obviously is asked concerning Christ during his life on earth. Although it has seemed best to insert a new title, the question is still helping to put Guerric in relation to modern theologians. When a book was placed on the Index,

58. Ser. 28, 3rd for Annunciation: 6; II, 53.

readers were more attracted to it; and I have to confess that I
became all the more interested in Guerric's text, when I
found that others had been so interested as to feel the need
of correcting it. It will be interesting now to place side by
side the earlier text which is attested by all the manuscripts
of the Igny recension, and the text with the interpolation
(indicated in capital letters), which is found in all manuscripts of the Clairvaux revision.[59] The middle recension is, if
the account of the critical edition is correct, a stage on the
way to this revision, and it always gives the inserted passage.

> So the Word feeds on the Word, the Son lives on himself,
> for as the Father has life in himself, so he has given to the
> Son to have life in himself.

> In another way, but yet
> with unspeakable beatitude
> and incomparable happi-
> ness, that Prince, sitting in
> the gate of the virginal
> womb, ate the bread of
> God's Word before the
> Lord.

> In another way, but yet
> with unspeakable beatitude
> THAT SOUL UNITED IN
> PERSON TO THE WORD
> HIMSELF FED UPON THE
> WORD; and with incompar-
> able happiness that Prince,
> sitting in the gate of the
> virginal womb, ate the
> bread of God's Word before
> the Lord.

So the text on the left — presumably the text which Guerric wrote — has not been read for centuries. The Latin has
passed out of the manuscript tradition, and has not been
printed before the edition of *Sources chrétiennes*. What is the
explanation of this? Has someone thought that the idea of
Christ receiving something, eating the Bread of the Word before the Lord, makes him subordinate in an heretical sense?
In the revised text it is not Christ, the Prince, who feeds upon
the Word, but the soul united to him, as though something
could be attributed to the soul as to a Person. The manuscript corrector has scrupulously added to "that soul":
"united into a person (*in personam*) to the Word himself."

59. See Introduction to edition: SCh 166: 74-79.

The printed text, reading "in a person" (*in persona*), is slightly inferior.

Christ feeds upon the Bread of the Word. I have criticized the attribution of this feeding to the soul; or at least I have suggested that it is not Guerric's natural way of speaking, and inferior to what he evidently said. At the same time I have been keenly aware of what Saint Thomas Aquinas said about one hundred years later: "The soul of Christ has infinite knowledge . . . the soul of Christ sees God more perfectly than any other creature."[60] He did not always speak so by any means: e. g. "Christ" (not "the soul of Christ") had the Knowledge of the blessed."[61] The answer may be that we are dealing with scholastic rather than patristic language, and that Guerric's corrector was under the influence of early pre-Thomist scholasticism. Also that an attribution to the soul of Christ is much more easily intelligible, sometimes even more convenient, in a scholastic context, when every element and function in the hypostatic union has been made the object of careful distinction and speculation. Guerric was no scholastic. We now see what Guerric said, and this is the way in which it came naturally to him to speak. That Prince is the Word made Flesh, God and Man, with our human nature, body and soul. Sitting in the gate of the Virgin's womb, eating the Bread of the Word before the Lord, he invites us to be his guests, and it is his delight to have us eating with him.

Did Christ in his human nature enjoy the beatific vision, even during his life on earth? The words last quoted from Guerric, and the history of the text, have a bearing upon the question. The introduction — "In another way" — seems to indicate quite clearly that we are now concerned with human knowledge. What about the "unspeakable beatitude and incomparable happiness"? Does this mean what we call beatific knowledge? It may well seem so, for it is difficult to think of this as something less than what Christ, as God, has given to the angels: "He who as God is born eternally to give blessedness to the angels."[62]

60. Thomas Aquinas, *Summa theologica,* 3, 10, 3.4.
61. *Ibid.* 3, 9, 2.
62. Ser. 6, 1st for Christmas: 1; I, 37.

Yet it may be better not to use this text to prove that Guerric attributed beatific knowledge to Christ. For we read in the next place that we are to use our silence with Christ in the same way. The Lord will be delighted if we will eat his Bread with him — evidently in this life. It is almost as if Christ has a need which we can satisfy: "He who feeds you will himself be fed in you." Mary is brought to the same supper table; like her we are to ponder these things in our heart. Putting this last into another language: it is what the theologians will call "acquired knowledge."

Even if we should be hesitant about the kind of knowledge which is meant in this and other texts of the Annunciation sermon, yet it would seem that Guerric, if he were asked at any time, would attribute to Christ on earth the knowledge which the blessed enjoy in heaven.

His idea of a consummation in a face to face vision is clear enough. "You have so many lamps burning within you. When the lamp of this life has gone out, the light of unending life will begin to shine. . . . No more need of the daily changing of sun and moon to light your way: the Lord will be for you an everlasting light."[63] It is yet clearer in the conclusion of another Purification sermon, where the stages of spiritual progress are described for us: "Finally, from the beginning of this faith, you will pass on . . . at last from that which is but an appearance and an image to that which rests in the truth of his face, in the face of his truth . . . you will stand before the Lord in Jerusalem, living in his beholding, looking upon him without end face to face."[64]

But Christ is this beatitude for himself. Even if the third Annunciation sermon is not used to prove this point, it may well be in Guerric's mind, when he says that the one who eats and the Bread which is eaten are the same. He says elsewhere: "he is his own beatitude." If anywhere Christ was abandoned and forsaken, it was in his Passion, and even theologians who have attributed the beatific vision to him have thought of it

63. Ser. 15, 1st for Purification: 5; I, 105.
64. Ser. 19, 5th for Purification: 6; I, 132.

being withdrawn at this time. Yet it is in the context of the Passion that Guerric is speaking: "The desire of our soul, the most comely among the sons of men, is put before them today, now in one guise, now in another . . . in the one glorious, in the other suffering; in the one for our veneration, in the other for our pity; if indeed he is to be pitied. It was because he deigned to pity that he took misery upon himself, using such misery to give mercy to those who were in misery; not that he might crave mercy from the miserable, he who IS HIMSELF HIS OWN BEATITUDE."[65]

"THE LORD OF HOSTS is with us." This must suffice as an attempt to analyse Guerric's teaching on the Incarnation of the Son of God. One might have followed an entirely different method, e. g. taken headings and propositions from the *Summa* of Saint Thomas or from a modern theologian, and placed under them whatever texts from Guerric were thought relevant. No thesis on a mediaeval writer can be the same thing as the author himself, but this would have been such a travesty that I would have refused to undertake it. Some analysis and conceptual arrangement there must be; but it is not easily done. The difficulty is that any paragraph is so rich that it contains many aspects of revealed truth.

For convenience one might take something readily accessible: the third volume of the *Sacrae Theologiae Summa* published by Spanish Jesuits, even though now, after less than twenty years, it would be considered out of date. Under *The Incarnate Word* here are some theses: "The one primary motive of the Incarnation was the redemption of the human race. . . . The union of the Word incarnate did not come about in a nature. . . . The union of the Word incarnate came about in a person, etc.. . . . The human nature of Christ is not a person for this reason: that it lacks a substantial manner of subsistence, etc.. . . . The union of a human nature with the Person of the Word implies a certain substantial mode in the humanity, etc."[66] Undoubtedly some texts of a mediaeval author like ours could have been brought into relation with

65. Ser. 31, 3rd for Palm Sunday: 1; II, 66.
66. *Sacrae Theologiae Summa* III (Madrid: B. A. C., 1956).

such propositions; but, if Guerric had been, so to say, stretch-
ed upon this rack, would the result have been a thesis on
Guerric? Also, one can read such a treatise as that for hour
after hour and find hardly any reference to ourselves. There
is not intention of criticizing it, since in its own field it is
excellent and would never have been written if it had not
served a need. But the contrast may serve to emphasize the
difference in the *genre littéraire* and the approach. Nor let it
be said that such a treatise is theology, and Guerric's sermons
are not.

Guerric of Igny takes for granted the teaching handed
down to him and then develops richly several aspects of the
central Mystery: the Word made Flesh. This is chiefly by the
allegorical exegesis of Sacred Scripture, the use of figure and
symbol. The Mother of the Word Incarnate is there all the
time, as she should be; yet another chapter has been devoted
to the exposition of types which concern her more particularly. The twelfth century has not seen all the development
which we have seen of the Church's doctrine concerning
Mary. If it has not been so much preoccupied as we have
been in later times with her entire freedom from original sin,
her bodily Assumption into heaven, rather less with the manner of her co-operation in our Redemption; it has yet reflect-
ed very profoundly upon her — perhaps more profoundly
than ourselves — upon Mary as the Mother of God and of our
Redeemer, indeed the Mother of our Redemption, that is,
upon the most central truths which the Church has ever
taught concerning her.

It was not the Father who assumed our Nature, not the
Spirit, but the Word. Without trying to scrutinize unduly the
reason for God's choice, or even its congruity, we can remember that the Word is God's infinite Knowledge in which all
things which will ever come to be already have life. Now we
have among us one who is God and Man, and his first activity
is knowing the Father. Divine and human knowledge cannot
be confused, but it is the One Person who knows. An author
like ours is far more concerned with this One who knows
than with distinguishing his kinds and degrees of knowledge.

In the theology of light, the heritage into which Guerric enters,[67] we make our progress towards God by knowing him more fully.[68] This is a participation of the knowledge which Christ has as both God and Man. The next part of our discussion will be concerned with our Redemption and will pass on to reflect upon some aspects of our Sanctification. But already it has been impossible to leave this aside when speaking of Christ's principal work: knowing the Father and inviting us to know with him.

In this life our thought must be to a greater or less extent conceptual and divided. Yet there is — and the consummation of our knowledge will be to gaze upon him — the "Word of the Father, which although it is simple contains in itself the reason and form of every divine word."[69]

67. Introduction; SCh 166:42-68.
68. Ser. 19, 5th for Purification: 6; I, 132.
69. Ser. 28, 3rd for Annunciation: 6; II, 53.

"Christ Jesus, Our Sanctification and Redemption"

CHAPTER NINE

# THE PURPOSE: MEDIATION AND REDEMPTION

MEDIATION—acting or standing between—does not need to be further explained for the moment. "Redemption" means buying back or ransoming one who is held captive. "If you are led into captivity or sold, here I am, sell me and redeem yourself at my cost"; so says Guerric.[1] "Satisfaction" suggests that an injury has been inflicted and that justice demands some reparation. Supposing original sin, it will be involved in a Redemption theology. If Christ redeemed the human race, it does not immediately follow that each member is justified, sanctified, raised to a sharing of the divine life. In other words objective Redemption must become subjective. It seems necessary to make these very elementary distinctions, although we shall not expect to find them clearly formulated in a Guerric of Igny. We shall repeatedly be speaking of our redemption and renewal. To apply the word Redemption to those who are in no need of such deliverance, as Saint Bernard does when he speaks of the redemption of the angels,[2] is to extend the ordinary and natural meaning of the term.

Whatever be the *genre littéraire* of the early chapters of Genesis, it never occurs to a twelfth-century writer like Guerric to ask in what sense they are historical. He is none the worse for this, since the profound meaning of the third chapter is clear enough. Man has walked with God in Paradise, but

1. Ser. 29, 1st for Palm Sunday: 1; II, 56.
2. Bernard, *On the Song of Songs* 22:5-6; OB 1:132; CF 7.

has been estranged and lost the divine friendship. God allows sin; but why? We may answer: that it may be transcended by his grace. He preferred to let this be, and to make it the occasion for a still greater manifestation of his love, a more wonderful communication of himself. "Oh truly necessary sin of Adam. . . . Oh happy fault . . . ," is not mere rhetoric after all. Guerric maintains that the redemption of the fallen was a more sublime work than their first creation: "Truly 'the free gift is not like the sin,' because where sin increased there grace abounds all the more, not only forgiving sin but heaping up the merits of virtue. Redemption has raised the fallen up again, but has raised them higher than ever they were by their first creation."[3] Saint Bernard has said already: "You have made all things for yourself, O God . . . But there is something else that moves me, arouses and inflames me even more. Good Jesus, the chalice you drank, the price of our redemption, makes me love you more than all the rest."[4]

### THE MEDIATOR

If God and man were estranged, there was need for reconciliation; a bridge had to be built. A Mediator was needed, and the one supremely qualified to do the office of Mediator was both God and Man. At Christmas Guerric is reminded of Saint Leo's words: "True God and true Man are blended together into the oneness of the Lord, that we might have what our healing called for, one and the same Mediator of God and men. . . ."[5] Guerric himself expressed it thus: "The art of mercy has blended God's beatitude and man's misery, making them one in the Mediator. . . ."[6] (The quotation is deliberately truncated for the moment.) God was so skilled in the art of mercy that he brought the divine beatitude and human misery together, blended them into the oneness effected by a Mediator.

3. Ser. 38, 1st for Pentecost: 1; II, 110.
4. Bernard, *On the Song of Songs*, 20:2; OB 1:115; CF 4:148.
5. Leo, 1st sermon for Christmas: 2; SCh 22:72.
6. Ser. 6, 1st for Christmas: 1; I, 38.

Through Christ's mediation we are to be led to the eternal wisdom of the Blessed Trinity. This underlies the accustomed conclusion of each sermon. The one just quoted ends with these words: " . . . in the complete accord of our lives and voices, 'out of the mouths of babes and sucklings' shall perfect praise be given to the Babe and Suckling, our Lord Jesus Christ, to whom with the Father and the Holy Spirit be praise and rejoicing throughout endless ages. Amen."[7] These conclusions are not mere stereotyped formulae; they are beautifully woven into the thought and expression which has led up to them. One more may be quoted, first because it puts Christ before us as the means or the Way, secondly because, although it is attested by all the manuscripts, the Cistercian Father Series has been the first edition to make it available to English readers: "These are the footsteps, brethren, in which we may follow Christ in the form of a slave, and come in the end to see him in the form of God, in which he lives and reigns for ever and ever."[8]

### MARY, THE MEDIATRESS

When Guerric writes of Christ as Mediator, he cannot forget Bernard's sermons, which he has read with care. Who could forget the conclusion of that fourth Assumption sermon: "Let him not speak of your mercy, blessed Virgin, if there be any who has called upon it in his need and found it lacking. . . ."[9] Bernard has been yet more explicit, and has given Mary the title of Mediatress: "We need a mediator to this Mediator: we shall find none better for this than Mary. . . . The Moon, prostrate beneath your feet, makes you its own, giving you no rest as it cries out to you, its Mediatress before the Sun of Justice. . . ."[10] She is then the Mediatress to the Mediator. "He willed that we should have all through Mary." How much is involved in this audacious phrase? At least this

7. Ser. 6, 1st for Christmas: 4; I, 41.
8. Ser. 29, 1st for Palm Sunday: 3; II, 58. Compare the truncated text in PL 185:130C.
9. Bernard, 4th for Assumption: 8; OB 5:249; CF 31.
10. Bernard, Sunday in Octave of Assumption: 2-15; OB 5:263-274; CF 31.

much: Christ is Man, but he is also God, and we may be overwhelmed by his majesty. "Would you have an Advocate to plead your cause before him? Turn to Mary."[11]

Without using in this particular place the word either "mediation" or "mediatress," Guerric tells us plainly that through Mary the grace of Christ came to Elizabeth and to the Baptist. "In truth Mary was 'full of grace.' The God of all grace was clearly in her, when from his liberality the generous gift of grace flowed with magnificent abundance first to his Mother, then from his Mother to John and from John to his parents."[12]

By occasion of Christ's title and office of Mediator it has been fitting to speak of Mary as Mediatress. But she exercises this function most obviously in the application of the grace won for us, as we should say, in subjective redemption. It has been impossible to separate the strict theological notions of redemption and sanctification.[13]

Here are the persons and the functions as Guerric sees them in the first Purification procession: "The Child and his Mother, Jesus and Mary . . . the Lord and the Lady . . . the Mediator and the Mediatress."[14] Finally Mary's exaltation is described as follows in the first Assumption sermon: " . . . let the Mother then contemplate nothing above herself but her Son, the Queen gaze in wonder at nothing above herself but

11. Bernard, Our Lady's Birthday: 7; OB 5:279; CF 31. While I think that Guerric had remembered Bernard and followed him closely, again I do not wish to suggest that Bernard was his only source. For the expansion of the mediation theme he may be indebted to Ambrose Autpert: *Adest . . . dies valde venerabilis,* n. 11; PL 39:2133-2144. This was known to him under the name of Saint Augustine.

12. Ser. 40, 1st for St John Baptist: 2; II, 124.

13. This would be the place to expand upon Mary's part in our sanctification as described in Ser. 52:3, 2nd for Our Lady's Birthday; II, 200-201: "She desires to form her Only-Begotten in all her sons by adoption. Although they have been brought to birth by the word of truth, nevertheless she brings them forth every day by desire and loyal care until they reach the stature of the perfect man, the maturity of her Son, whom she bore and brought forth once and for all." This has been done amply by De Wilde (See Introduction to this volume, p. []), and a summary account is given in our Introduction to the edition: CF 8, xxxiv-xxxvi.

14. Ser. 16, 2nd for Purification: 6; II, 111.

the King, our Mediatress offer veneration to none above herself but the Mediator alone. . . ."[15]

The title "Mediatress" is rightly used with caution, for it is one of those things which can lead to the excesses of superstition and sheer mariolatry. The Fathers of the second Vatican Council have been anxious to give a thoroughly balanced account and to place Mary where she belongs in the Mystery of Salvation. "Co-redemptress" is avoided. "Mediatress" is found: "This, however, is to be so understood that it neither takes away from nor adds anything to the dignity and efficacy of Christ the one Mediator."[16] The early Cistercians were troubled neither by excesses nor by reactions against them, and had no scruples when they spoke of a "mediatress," a "mediator to the Mediator." Steeped in Scripture, they could not but have been keenly aware of that most significant text: "There is one Mediator between God and men, the man Christ Jesus."[17] Once redeemed, all Christians are invited to share in Christ's timeless work of mediation and redemption; but this invitation is accorded by a supreme title to the one whom Guerric calls "the Mother of Redemption."[18]

IT IS DIFFICULT to maintain that Guerric belongs to a particular school of thought, as does Saint Anselm for instance, with regard to our Redemption, or that his ideas are either precise or original. Father Hilary Costello has devoted an article to the meaning of Redemption in Guerric's sermons. Although in this matter I have worked independently of him, I find myself in agreement with what he has expressed as follows: —

Before the twelfth century there were three theories to explain Christ's redemptive work. Little attempt was made

15. Ser. 47, 1st for Assumption: 7; II, 172 (The number 7 should introduce the paragraph at the top of this page).

16. Vatican II, Dogmatic Constitution on the Church, ch. 8: *The Blessed Virgin Mary*, n. 62; tr. M. Abbott - J. Gallagher, (New York: America Press, 1966), pp. 91-92.

17. 1 Tim 2:5.

18. Ser. 18, 4th for Purification: 1; I, 121.

to effect a theological fusion between them; they seem to
run parallel to one another in the minds of the Fathers, so
that they now stress one theory now another, as it suits
their purpose at the moment. The first of these theories has
been called "Divinisation by Assimilation."[19]

This must now occupy our attention. The idea, even though
it remains somewhat implicit, is central to Guerric's thought.
There is but one Mediator. Our human nature is raised up
simply because that Mediator has taken it as his own.


It was necessary to speak of Mary's part in mediation, and
this could be done only in the context of her Son's office and
work as Mediator. The theme was approached with a few
words from the first Christmas sermon, because the first concern was with the oneness effected by a Mediator (*in unita-
tem Mediatoris*). Here is the sentence in full, for there is
much more to be learned from it: "For this, the art of mercy
has blended God's beatitude and man's misery, making them
one in the Mediator, that by dint of the sacrament of this
unity, in virtue of his resurrection, beatitude may absorb
misery, life swallow up death, and the whole man pass glorified into fellowship with the divine nature."[20] This happens
by the power of Christ's resurrection; there is no mention of
his death, so that we have not the completeness of the corresponding passage in Saint Leo: " . . . that the one [of two
natures united in one Lord] might enable him to die, the
other to rise again."[21] Here once more are the principal oper-
ating words in Guerric: " . . . by dint of the sacrament of this
unity . . . pass glorified into fellowship with the divine nature." Man's elevation to a new life, his divinisation, seems to
be attributed simply to the "sacrament of unity," the union
of divine and human natures in the one Person of Christ. Are

19. Hilary Costello, "The Meaning of Redemption in the Sermons of Guerric of
Igny," *Cîteaux* 17 (1966), 281-308. Quotation from p. 287.
20. Ser. 6, 1st for Christmas: 1; I, 38.
21. Leo, 1st ser. for Christmas: 2; SCh 22:72.

we renewed, indeed redeemed, simply because Christ is God and Man? At the beginning of the same sermon we read: ". . . the Child is born to renew us . . .," and a little later: " . . . born of the Holy Spirit, immaculate from her who was immaculate, he set right the sins which we drew from our first beginning, and gave us the mysteries which should bring about our second birth."[22] The implication is found at the conclusion of this sermon: "So it shall be that as new-born babes we shall worthily praise the new-born infant Lord. . . ."[23] In the next we read: "ONCE HE WAS GIVEN TO THE WORLD SHAPED IN FLESH; and on certain days, at set times, he is offered to the faithful in the likeness of bread; the food, I mean, of his own Sacrament; but to his devoted friends he is quite often granted at unexpected moments by the taste of his Spirit. THE FIRST IS FOR OUR REDEMPTION, the second to sanctify, the third goes so far as to comfort us."[24]

Of some of these passages it may be said that obviously they have the Passion and Cross in view. But in the third Christmas sermon we have a passage which more clearly and categorically attributes our Resurrection and renewal to the Incarnation and birth of Jesus. Each of us has been born a sinner, but the birth of the Son of God has cancelled our illegitimacy. There was a bill of indictment against us; but this birth has withdrawn it: "Child Jesus, how your happy birth cries out for our love! It sets right the birth of each one of us, repairs his condition, reverses the judgment upon him, cancels the writ of condemnation drawn up against his nature. Is a man ashamed that he has been born for damnation? He can be blissfully reborn."[25] Then a few lines later: "Wondrous exchange indeed! That you should take flesh and bestow divinity."[26] These last words are valuable, for they indicate the source of this teaching. The attribution of our redemption

22. Ser. 6, 1st for Christmas: 1; I, 37-38.
23. Ibid.: 4; I, 41.
24. Ser. 7, 2nd for Christmas: 3; I, 46.
25. Ser. 8, 3rd for Christmas: 1; I, 48.
26. Ibid.

and renewal to the Incarnation itself was prevalent in some of the Eastern Fathers. Guerric has been recalling an antiphon which came into Western liturgies from the East, perhaps in the seventh century, and has been in the Cistercian ligurgy since the twelfth. It is little known in the West, so here it is in full: "O wondrous exchange! The Creator of the race of man has taken to himself a living body and deigned to be born of a Virgin. Without human seed he has come forth as man and bestowed on us his godhead."

Jean Rivière noted this Incarnationalist doctrine in several of the Eastern Fathers.[27] The Pseudo-Macarius, preaching on Our Lord's birth, is very close to Guerric, though it is impossible to demonstrate a real dependence: "The Lord is born today, men's life and salvation. Today God is reconciled with man, man with God. This is the day when all things created dance for joy. Today a road lies open for man to go to God; for God to come to man's soul."[28]

It is interesting to notice that we need not go so far back as the Middle Ages or the Greek Fathers to find what I have recalled this Incarnational doctrine, which taken simply at its face value seems to teach that we were redeemed, reconciled, raised to new life, by Christ's taking our human nature, quite apart from his death. "Taking on human nature, Christ bound the whole human race to himself as a family through a certain supernatural solidarity. . . ." These are the words of the second Vatican Council.[29] We need to use considerable discretion in putting Guerric aside this Council. If he is aware

27. Jean Rivière, *Dict. de Théol. Catholique* XIII, 2; article *Rédemption,* col. 1938. I cannot find much account of it, as I thought I might, in his extensive work *Le Dogme de la Rédemption au début du Moyen Age* (1934). Leclercq and Bonnes clearly attribute it to John of Fécamp: *Un maître de la vie spirituelle* (1946), p. 86: "S'il y a satisfaction, c'est l'Incarnation même qui la réalise: s'identifiant avec nous par amour, le Christ enlève l'obstacle qui séparait de Dieu notre nature pécheresse."

28. Pseudo-Macarius, hom. 52, n. 1; cf. n. 6; translated by Placide Deseille *L'Evangile au désert* (Paris, 1964); from critical edition by G. J L. Marriott, *Macarii anecdota* (Cambridge, 1918). But the christology of the Pseudo-Macarius seems to me confused and Monophysite.

29. Vatican II, *Decree on the Apostolate of the Laity,* n. 8; tr. W. Abbot and J. Gallagher, p. 498.

of the renewing value of the Incarnation, yet he gives only the germ of what will break into blossom and fruit centuries after his time. The Council teaches us also:

> He who is "the image of the invisible God" is himself the perfect man. To the sons of Adam he restores the divine likeness which had been disfigured from the first sin onward. Since human nature as he assumed it was not annulled, by that very fact it has been raised up to a divine dignity in our respect too. For by his Incarnation the Son of Man has united himself in some fashion with every man.

But we must attend carefully to the "in some fashion" (*quodammodo*), recalling "a certain solidarity" (*quadam solidarietate*) of the first quotation. It is good to have read and quoted up to this point, for the next paragraph warns us that we cannot stop short at an Incarnational theology of Redemption: "As an innocent lamb he merited life for us by the free shedding of his own blood."[30]

### REDEEMED BY CHRIST'S PASSION AND DEATH

However much is attributed to the Incarnation, the assumption by God of our human nature, as it were abstracting from the life, Passion and Death of Christ; a believing Christian could hardly maintain that we are redeemed by the Incarnation without the Passion and Death. The Chalice offered at the Last Supper holds the Blood of Christ which is going to be poured out for many for the remission of their sins.[31] The outstanding theme of the Epistle to the Hebrews is Christ entering once for all into the Holy Place, taking his own blood, thus securing an eternal redemption.[32] Whatever Saint Paul teaches about the virtue of the Resurrection, still he teaches quite clearly that Christ "was delivered up for our sins."[33] The elders fall down before the Lamb and say that he

---

30. Vatican II, *Pastoral Constitution on the Church in the Modern World,* n. 22; *ibid.* p. 220, 221.
31. Mt 26:28.
32. Heb 9:11-12.
33. Rom 4:25.

was killed, he redeemed them, bought them back to God in his Blood.[34]

There is no question of a writer so immersed in Scripture and Tradition as Guerric losing sight of this. We expect that the virtue of the Incarnation should be emphasized in the Christmas sermons. Christ comes to greet us and to wish us salvation, but of what avail is this if he does not effect and give it? "But you have given salvation, not only by greeting with the kiss of peace, in your union with their flesh, those whom you had greeted already with words of peace; but yet more: by doing the work of their salvation by your death on the cross." This is in an Advent sermon, where the principal theme is the coming of the Word made Flesh. A little later in the same sermon we read: " . . . he has brought about our salvation in his own blood, shedding it as the price, pouring it out for our drink."[35]

Mary has already received the title given to her Son: "Prince of Martyrs."[36] It is not immediately to the point here, for Guerric does not — any more than Bernard does — carry on the idea of mediation into that of co-redemption. He hardly approaches this concept, and the nearest thing to it is found in these words, put into Mary's mouth when she comes to die: "At the end came my Passion, too, when I beheld the mockery and torments of his Passion and Cross, learning through them, one by one, how truly Isaiah spoke of him when he said: 'Indeed he bore our ills and himself carried our pains'."[37]

### MADE ALIVE BY CHRIST'S RESURRECTION

Returning once again to the first Christmas sermon: human misery and divine bliss are brought together into the oneness effected by a Mediator. There is no mention here of Christ's death; but our deliverance and elevation to divine life come

34. Rev 5:9.
35. Ser. 2, 2nd for Advent: 2; I, 8-9.
36. Ambrose Autpert, *Adest . . . dies valde venerabilis,* n. 1; PL 39: 2130.
37. Ser. 48, 2nd for Assumption: 3; II, 175.

about "through the power of the Resurrection." This Resurrection is not merely a wreath of laurel placed on the brow of a victorious athlete; nor is it simply apologetic, to justify Christ's claim to be the Son of God; but it has an essential function in the mystery of our Redemption and renewal. Completing a quotation already made from the Epistle to the Romans: "He was delivered up for our sins and rose again for our justification." And again: "If Christ has not been raised, your faith is futile and you are still in your sins."[38] Guerric carries these words in his head, as he knows them from the Vulgate. He seems to make a combination of two Latin texts when he says that he is quoting the Apostle: *Christus enim mortuus est propter delicta nostra, et resurrexit propter iustificationem nostram*: "Christ died for our sins and rose again for our justification."[39]

This teaching of Scripture concerning the Resurrection as the culmination of the saving mystery is so clear that inevitably it runs through the tradition of the Fathers. It will be so onwards from Saint Ignatius of Antioch in the post-apostolic age. He seems never to mention the Passion and Death of Christ without explicit mention of his Resurrection. It must suffice to recall a text from his letter to the Romans: "I seek him who died on our behalf; my longing is for him who rose for us." Even here the preposition *hypér* with "died," as distinct from the *diá* with "rose," may be intended to stress that Christ's character of sacrificial victim was realized precisely in his death — the teaching evidently of the Epistle to the Hebrews.[40] There can be no question here of following such a subtle distinction of causality through the centuries; but Guerric says something very similar: "Wholly innocent of sin and therefore free from the debt of death, he yet paid it, dying of his own will on our behalf; and rising he has set us free from sin."[41]

38. 1 Cor 15:17.
39. A conflation of 1 Cor 15:3 and Rom 4:25.
40. Ignatius of Antioch, *Epistle to the Romans*: 6, 1; tr. J. H. Srawley (SPCK 1935), pp. 77.
41. Ser. 34, 2nd for Easter: 3; II, 88.

### OUR RENEWAL: THE FIRST AND SECOND RESURRECTION

This last quotation has brought us to the part of Guerric's writings in which he speaks most clearly of the power of Christ's resurrection in our spiritual renewal. The second and third Resurrection sermons are a commentary on the words, "Blessed and holy is he who shares in the first resurrection." Here the quotation ends for the moment, but the inspired text in fact continues: "Over such the second death has no power."[42] Saint Bernard teaches that the two resurrections correspond to two deaths, of the soul and of the body: the soul is raised by Christ's hidden coming, the body of his second coming in glory.[43] This recalls what Rupert of Deutz has said about two regenerations: "The first regeneration is the grace of Baptism, whereby we are reborn of water and the Holy Spirit; but the second or last regeneration is the bodily resurrection of the dead."[44] Now for Guerric, while the meaning of the two regenerations or resurrections is the same, there is a noteworthy difference of expression and even of thought; for he attributes all to the bodily resurrection of Christ: " 'Rising from the dead, the first fruits of those who have fallen asleep' Christ both has brought about for us the first resurrection, by the sacrament of his own, and after the example of that same resurrection will bring about for us the second." See here that the second and final resurrection is fashioned after an exemplar. What is essential, our being raised to the sharing of divine life, is expressed by something more intimate and profound: a "sacrament" or "mystery." "The first resurrection is that of souls, when he raises them together with himself to newness of life; the second will be that of bodies, when he forms this humbled body of ours anew, moulding it into the image of his glorified body."[45] This resurrection of the soul is the type, prefiguring, demonstration and even cause of the resurrection of the body.

42. Rev 20:6.
43. Bernard, *De Diversis* 116; OB 6-1:393.
44. Rupert of Deutz, *On Joel,* book 1; PL 168:232B.
45. Ser. 34, 2nd for Easter: 1; II, 86.

In this same paragraph our two resurrections are intertwin-
ed with another twofold resurrection: of the Head and of the
Body. As our first resurrection is the proof and the cause of
the second, just so: "The first resurrection of our Head, the
Lord Jesus Christ, is the cause and the proof of the second
resurrection, which will be that of his whole Body." Guerric
has learned of both from the pages of Saint Augustine. In
*The City of God* — and certainly elsewhere — he has read:
"There are two resurrections, the first (that is now) of the
soul, preventing the second death; the latter (future) of the
body, sending some into the second death, and others into
the life that despises and excludes all death whatsoever."[46]
He is also familiar with Augustine's Commentary on the
Psalms, where he has read of the resurrection of Head and
Body: "We know that the Christian's resurrection is already
accomplished in our Head, and is still to come in the members. For the Head of the Church is Christ; the members of
Christ are the Church. What has gone before in the Head will
follow in the Body."[47]

We have come thus far under the title "Redemption," re-
stricting ourselves to those who have needed deliverance, but
still applying this term very broadly: redemption not only
objective but also subjective; the regeneration and renewal
involved in the first resurrection, even the glorious second
resurrection — the *Eschaton*. In another terminology this
would have been: *Redemption — Grace — the Last Things*.
Is any apology needed? We could have been careful to separate these into clearly distinct sections and categories. But in
fact the process is entirely continuous. A Guerric of Igny
does not speculate in the abstract; he is close enough to
reality to see the work of salvation as it is. For him Redemption leads straight into Justification, that is, the renewal

46. Augustine, *The City of God*, book 20, ch. 6; Everyman's Library, vol. 2 (n.
983), p. 276.
47. Augustine, *Commentary on Ps.* 65, n. 1; CCL 39:838; tr. J. H. Newman,
*Exposition on the Book of Psalms: St. Augustine,* LF, 3:271 (Ps.66). Cf. on Ps.
129, n. 7; CCL 40:1894-1895; tr. *ibid.,* 6:69 (ps 130). Gregory the Great, *Homilies on the Gospels,* 21, nn. 2.6; PL 78:1171A-1172D. *Homilies on Ezekiel,* bk 2,
hom. 8, n.5; CCL142:339.

which he sees as the first resurrection; the first leads straight to the second, the raising of the body and unending bliss. He would find it grossly artificial and unreal to speak of one and to say that the other belonged to his next chapter. They are one: the Mystery of our Salvation. Without confusing one notion with another, we may do best to see this Mystery — already present, we have noticed, in the Incarnation of the Word — through Guerric's eyes as a single whole, and to follow without pause or interruption in his footsteps.

An objective study cannot be confined to those elements in Guerric's teaching which the Church, and we ourselves, have made our own. We do not claim that his contribution is highly original; rather he is a faithful witness to what has gone before him, for nearly everything which he says has been drawn from the Fathers of the Church. Not that he repeats slavishly or compiles an anthology; he has assimilated for himself the ideas which have come down to him, and he is a master of the language and of the style in which he gives new expression to them. Besides everything recorded so far, he passes on theories which Tradition has quietly dropped to one side, notions which even seem bizarre at our stage of the development of doctrine. We cannot pass them over, if we are to give an authentic account of Guerric of Igny and of those early Fathers of the Church who were his sources.

### ALL HIDDEN FROM THE DEVIL

First may be quoted the passage in which our Redemption is most explicitly of all attributed to the Passion and Death of Christ:

But whoever is that blessed and true Israel should know ... Christ has purged away his sins. "Making atonement for sins" through the blood of his Cross, he achieved the greatest triumph over princedoms and powers there where his strength was hidden. It was hidden, but not lost, for crucified through weakness he was alive by God's power. It was hidden, but it was not idle, because by his crucifixion he crucified the old man in all the elect. He crucified the world to Paul and Paul to the world. Finally he crucified the tyrant of this world and all the ministers of his long-standing tyranny.[48]

The "hidden" theme calls for first attention: "He achieved the greatest triumph over princedoms and powers there where his strength was hidden. It was hidden, but not lost... It was hidden, but it was not idle..." There is nothing remarkable in this, for obviously the godhead of Christ was hidden in his Crucifixion; but there is more than may appear at the first reading.

From whom was the godhead hidden? Above all from the Devil. Here is the meaning of the Silence in which all had to be accomplished. It is "a dead secret," as we should say in colloquial English; *sub secreto* in the divine council chamber. If by some accident the Devil should find it out, he might ruin everything. This has some foundation in the words of Saint Ignatius of Antioch: "The prince of this world did not know the secret of Mary's virginity and motherhood; just so he did not know the secret of the Lord's death."[49] From this time onwards, until the Redemption doctrine of Saint Anselm is generally accepted, the "secret" is classical. Ignatius is quoted by Origen, and the text of Origen is rendered into Latin by Saint Jerome.[50] The very Doctor of the Incarnation, Saint Leo the Great, in one of his best known sermons, says that the devil deceived men; it was only just that he himself should be deceived by God's secret strategy. Christ could have taken our flesh without being born of a woman; but there was a reason why he should be so born, and why the virginal conception and motherhood should be veiled in secrecy: "Beloved: Christ's very choosing to be born of a Virgin was surely not without a profound motive? This was done that the devil might remain ignorant of the salvation which had been born to the race of man. The spiritual design lay hid, that he might see this Man a man like others,

48. Ser. 30, 2nd for Palm Sunday: 2; II, 60.

49. Ignatius of Antioch, *Epistle to Ephesians*, 19:1; tr. J. H. Srawley (SPCK, 1935), p. 50. But the idea chiefly underlying these words is that of inscrutable designs and ineffable godhead.

50. Origen, 6th homily on Luke; PG 13:1815A. Jerome; PL 26:230-231. Jerome recalls this again in his commentary on Matthew, book 1, ch. 2; *ibid.* 24B.

and so think he had been born in the same way as all the rest."[51]

If Guerric needed to be reminded of this, Saint Bernard would be there to remind him constantly. This "Sacrament of the divine counsel" has to be hidden from the prince of this world (the very phrase of Saint Ignatius). God need not fear that the Devil will have power to hinder his designs; but it is fitting that the one who brought our ruin by deceiving a woman should now be deceived by a woman.[52] "Christ plunged himself more closely and more profoundly into man's universal misery, lest the devil's sharp eye should discern this sacrament of mercy."[53] In Isaiah's vision the Lord's feet are veiled by the wings of the Seraphim, so that the enemy may not know his unsearchable ways. "I think the Lord's feet were veiled, so that the devil might have the Lord of glory crucified without knowing what he did."[54] When Bernard insisted that none of the angels knew the details of God's plan before the Annunciation made by Gabriel, he was criticized, but defended his opinion at some length in a letter to Hugh of Saint Victor.[55] In fact this whole idea seems to reach its final elaboration among the Cistercians, even when Saint Anselm has already written his *Cur Deus homo.* Saint Aelred thinks that Christ's purpose in letting himself be tempted by the devil, being hungry as though in need, sleeping in the boat, going upon the cross to die, is to deceive the devil into thinking that he is a mere man. There even seems to be a tinge of docetism implied in all this, as though it were unnatural and contradictory for the Word Incarnate (like "his brethren in every respect") to hunger or to sleep.[56] In another place Aelred suggests that the Devil recognized that Christ was God before the Crucifixion and tried to prevent the saving death through the intervention of Pilate's wife.[57]

51. Leo, 2nd for Christmas: 3; SCh 22:80.
52. Bernard, *On the Praises of the Virgin Mother* 2: 13; OB 4:30; CF 43.
53. *Id.*, Wednesday of Holy Week: 10; OB 5:63; CF 22.
54. *Id.*, 1st Sunday of November 5: 11; OB 5:325; CF 22.
55. *Id.*, *On Baptism*: 18-21; PL 182:1042-6.
56. Aelred, *Jesus at the Age of Twelve*: 25; CCL Cont Med 1:272; CF 2:33.
57. *Id. Rule of Life for a Recluse*: 31; CCL Cont Med 1:670; CF 2:89. Cf. *Sermones inediti*, ed. C. H. Talbot (Rome: Editiones Cistercienses, 1952), *Sermo beate virginis*, p. 138.

### THE BAIT AND HOOK: THE DEVIL'S RIGHTS

It must be thought that this has gone far from Guerric of Igny, and that too much is being made of his few words. However, it is certain that he has all this teaching in mind. Not that he has read Saint Aelred; but he has followed Saint Bernard closely. Anyhow, this idea of hiding from the Devil is still common property, even though by the time of Guerric, still more Aelred, it is becoming out of date in the schools. Guerric's words can now be taken up where they were left:

> In the last place he crucified the tyrant of this world and all the ministers of his long-standing tyranny. To be sure he concealed the hook under the bait by hiding his strength under weakness. So that murderer who from the beginning thirsted for human blood, rushing blindly upon weakness encountered strength; he was bitten in the act of biting, transfixed as he grasped at the Crucified. Thanks be to your cross and nails, Lord Jesus. I see the jaws of that serpent pierced through, so that those who were swallowed may pass through them. He who was confident that the Jordan would flow into his mouth is in a frenzy of anger, because he has largely lost that river which he swallowed. They have come to us from those jaws, who join us today as we hymn the cross's noble and splendid triumph.[58]

Here is the metaphor of the bait and the hook. The Devil saw a human nature and entered into combat with the man before him. The human nature was a bait, and he found his jaws pierced with a hook. He tried to fight against the God whom he had never discerned. This is simply a picturesque development of the secrecy theme which has been outlined from Saint Ignatius onwards.

It is based on a passage near the end of the book of Job, which, as the Western Fathers knew it, reads approximately as follows: "Behold Behemoth, which I made as I made you . . . See: he will swallow the river, and not be surprised. He is confident that the Jordan will flow into his mouth. Before his eyes, one will take him with a hook, and will pierce his nostrils with stakes. Will you be able to draw out

58. Ser. 30, *2nd for Palm Sunday:* 3; II, 60-61.

Leviathan with a hook, and will you bind his tongue with a cord? Will you put a ring in his nostrils, or pierce his jaw with a bracelet."[59]

The allegorical interpretation of this passage to the Devil is insinuated by Origen[60] and is found in Saint Gregory of Nyssa.[61] Saint Augustine says: "(The Devil) snatched the food as bait in a trap."[62] But Guerric is most likely to have assimilated the idea from one of the homilies on the gospels by Saint Gregory the Great. This is one of the best known passages which is to our purpose, and has had a far-reaching influence on the Redemption theology of the Middle Ages. For this reason it may be quoted at some length:

"Will you take Leviathan with a hook? " . . . On a hook a bait is shown, but a prong is hidden. So the almighty Father took him with a hook, for to destroy him he sent his only begotten Son incarnate. The flesh, subject to suffering, could be seen; the godhead, above all suffering, could not. When the serpent bit the bait of the body, through the hands of persecutors, he was pierced by the hook of the godhead. First of all, when miracles were worked, he had acknowledged Christ as God, but fell into doubting when he saw that he was able to suffer. The hook, as it were, pierced the serpent's jaws, when he came hungry to devour the flesh which was hanging there for all to see. The godhead lay hidden in the time of the Passion, but it was the godhead which killed the serpent. This serpent was caught by the hook of the Incarnation, seeking there the bait of the body, transfixed by the prong of the divinity. The humanity was there to draw on the one who came to devour; the divinity was there to pierce him. Weakness lay uncovered to entice; strength lay hidden to pierce the jaws of the one who laid hold of the prey. So the serpent was caught with a hook, done in by that on which he had closed his

59. Job 40:10, 18-21 (Vulgate numbering).
60. Origen, *First Principles*, book 1, ch. 5, n. 5; PG 11:164; tr. G. W. Butterworth (New York: Harper and Row, 1966).
61. Gregory of Nyssa, *Catechetical Sermon* 24; PG 45:64-65; tr. J. H. Srawley (London: SPCK, 1917).
62. Augustine, Sermon 263:1; PL 38:1210; tr. M. S. Muldowney, FC 38:392. Cf. Jerome, on this place of Job; PL 26:786BC.

mouth. He lost those mortals whom he had a right to hold; because he presumed to lure into death that Immortal One, over whom he had no rights at all.[63]

This passage from Gregory serves a double purpose. It is a source and a clear explanation of the bait-and-hook theory found in Guerric and in other Cistercian writers.[64] At the same time it brings us right into the Redemption theory which prevailed in the Middle Ages, based upon rights which the Devil was supposed to have acquired over man. This is summed up in his last sentence: "He lost those mortals whom he had a right to hold; because he presumed to lure into death that Immortal One, over whom he had no right at all." The ideas of secrecy and bait-and-hook are bound up with that of the Devil's rights. He had acquired these when man fell into his power at the beginning. When he brought about the death of Christ, he thought he was taking only what was his due. But that victim was God, over whom he had no right at all. He now forfeited whatever rights he had been able to exercise over the human race. Men were now exempt from his tyranny. If Guerric has anything original it is the personal touch, the intimacy of his expression: "Thanks be to your cross and nails, Lord Jesus."

It may well be said that theories such as this which has been outlined are neither scriptural nor can have any interest or relevance for us of today.[65] Whatever truth there is in this, it seems a mistake to pass them over in a positive theological study. If we are to draw profit from writers like Bernard,

---

63. Gregory the Great, *Homily on the Gospels* 25: 8; PL 76:1194-5.

64. So as not to multiply quotations I simply refer to Aelred, *In die Pasche*, with excerpt from another recension (a); and *In Synodo, De Pastore . . .; Sermones inediti*, ed. Talbot, pp. 95-96; also to Amedeus of Lausanne, hom. 5:88; 8:113; SCh 72:144, 214; CF 18.

65. It is only to be expected that authors who speak of the devil's rights should have supported them with scriptural texts. Hilary of Poitiers thought they were implied in words of the Psalmist, put into the mouth of Christ, over whom the rights were no longer valid: "They have prevailed, my enemies who persecute me unjustly; I was condemned to pay back what I had never stolen" (Commentary on ps. 68:4; PL 9:474-5). St John Chrysostom discerned the devil's rights in the law of sin which held us captive, sold under sin, until Christ condemned sin in the flesh (Rom. 7:6; 8:4. Chrysostom on this epistle: homily 13:5; PG 60:514).

Guerric, or Aelred — and who can deny that we have much to learn from them? — we must see them in their historical background, and have some idea, however summary or briefly stated, of what was being said and thought in the environment of their upbringing. How do they stand in relation to this? Have they passed on from it something which is of lasting value? [66]

SUMMARY OF GUERRIC'S IDEAS

Guerric is so familiar with scriptural and with many patristic texts, that he cannot attribute redemption to Christ's death taken quite alone, as though his Resurrection were simply a reward conferred upon him for the redemption completed on Calvary. He has read so often that the Incarnation of the Word has brought about our renewal, that he cannot think of the Incarnation simply as something which is necessary in order to provide the one who alone can be offered as a victim of a redeeming sacrifice. However clearly Scripture teaches that we are redeemed by the shedding of Christ's blood, it is none the less clear that we are redeemed by his death with his Incarnation, life and Resurrection. Although Guerric makes no mention of the *recapitulatio (anakephalaiôsis)* emphasized especially by Saint Irenaeus,[67] he is aware that Christ sums up and represents the human race from Adam onwards. In the Person of the Word Incarnate all hu-

---

66. This is the place at which to appreciate in more explicit terms the monumental work of Jean Rivière, published in 1934. He devoted more than five hundred pages to a study of Redemption theology in a particular period: *Le Dogme de la Rédemption au début du Moyen Age.* This must show how many elements and intricacies there were in the debate, which are either expressed in very summary form or else left aside in such a limited study as my own. Hilary Costello in an article mentioned above, note 19, p.110, has given Guerric a place in the currents of thought (or perhaps a detachment from the currents of thought) which were discernible in the twelfth century. I am interested to see that he has found, as I have myself, that in presenting Guerric to possible readers, one cannot deal with objective redemption apart from subjective, the application to ourselves of what Christ has effected, the present work of our sanctification. He has made much of the Resurrection sermons.

67. Irenaeus, *Against heresies* V, 21, 10F; SCh 34:370f; tr. J. Keble. LF (1872), p. 498.

manity can deal with God on equal terms: "already my being is with you."[68] A contemporary theologian even goes so far as to speak of Christ being redeemed.[69] Being without sin either original or actual — even without the "debt owed by nature," and here is the immense difference between himself and his Mother — he had no need of any redemption.[70] Yet he was not simply one person, but the whole of humanity summed up in one person — we are only following the teaching of Saint Irenaeus. He *is* the whole of humanity, not simply in the juridical but in the real sense. Schillebeeckx speaks more than once of Christ as the "representatively redeemed"; himself the Redemption which gives, but also receives and accepts in our name. Saint Thomas Aquinas says several times that Christ's humanity is "justified" in order that it may be the source of our sanctification.[71] Here, on the level of scholastic and modern speculation, we can see how essential is the Incarnation in the Mystery of our Redemption; and it is not difficult to understand why Tradition has often spoken as though the Incarnation alone redeemed us. As for Christ's saving death, it is the co-natural manifestation of man's sinful and culpable separation from God; not simply a penalty enjoined from without, which God could equally well have replaced by something else. Yet death is for man a penalty. In the death of Jesus Christ and in his resurrection, man's fault, original and personal, is both manifested and overcome.[72] Christ has now realized representatively, like Adam before him, the life destiny of the human race, though this time by means of a restoration. Certainly this "representative" theme is not so explicit in Guerric as it is in later writers. Rather it is implicit in what we have read about the renewal of our nature by its hypostatic union with the godhead.

68. Ser. 1, 1st for Advent: 1; I, 1.

69. E. Schillebeeckx, *Mary the Mother of the Redemption*, (New York: Sheed and Ward, 1964), pp. 62-64.

70. Cf. Aquinas, *Summa theol.* 3a pars, q. 27, a. 2 ad 2.

71. Not all the places given by Schillebeeckx are convincing. I would retain 3a pars, q. 34, 1 (c., ad 3), a. 3; q. 8, a. 5.

72. Cf. Karl Rahner, "Current Problems in Christology" in *Theological Investigations* I (Baltimore: Helicon, 1961), pp. 192-197.

This is the conclusion of a section which has represented the Redemption doctrine of Guerric of Ignay and of others before him. Christ saves us, raises us up to divine life, by becoming one of us. We are redeemed by the shedding of his Blood; we are renewed by his Resurrection. It is for a reader to judge whether all that is best in scholastic and modern speculation is perfectly in line with all that is best in Guerric of Igny and in the earlier Fathers.

SAINT ANSELM

One of the merits of Saint Anselm is that in his *Why God became Man* he renews the theology of the Redemption, especially by laying aside elements which are incompatible with revealed truth, such as that of rights which were acquired by the Devil, so that God himself had to resort to secrecy and a skilful ruse in order to save man from his dominion. In consideration of God's supreme justice it was necessary that the order disturbed by man should be restored by an act of reparation, freely made by the culprit and freely accepted by the one offended. As satisfaction for a wrong committed it should have a penal character. Due reparation to an infinite God could be made only by an act of infinite value. Man, finite as he is, could never make such a reparation by himself. But Christ, both God and man, could act as man's representative and could also make reparation by an act of infinite value.[73] Through the authority of Saint Thomas Aquinas this teaching has become more familiar to us than any other.[74]

CONCLUSION FOR OURSELVES

If Guerric ever read the *Cur Deus Homo,* I have been unable to find any trace of it in his sermons. Like other Cistercians, he was content to accept the traditional themes, without much speculation or effort to reconcile and synthe-

73. Anselm, *Cur Deus Homo,* SCh 91; tr. S. W. Deane (La Salle, Illinois: Open Court Pub., 1962).
74. Aquinas, The teaching is constant throughout the third part of the *Summa.* Q 48, a. 2, is particularly relevant.

size them. What of ourselves in the late twentieth century? The magisterium has spoken of "satisfaction," but in so doing has not defined the scholastic satisfaction theory.[75] Saint Anselm's teaching was acceptable when it was given, in the light of juridical notions and environment then prevailing; it is indeed an interesting example of the influence of the organization of Canon Law upon the emergence of new theological trends. It is undoubtedly true and acceptable to us, as far as it goes. But surely Saint Thomas, like Saint Anselm before him, would admit that it does not give a complete account of the mystery of our Salvation; that, like any such reduction to human formulae, it contains a strongly anthropomorphic element, and could give rise to misunderstandings. If God loves us, that is not only because the infinite satisfaction has been made; but rather with his infinite love he has taken the initiative. There seems to be only an extrinsic connection with some of the effects of our Redemption: resurrection, glory, the transformation of the cosmos. It is not evident that the teaching takes sufficient account of the Incarnation as such, which all through Tradition is seen as uniting the human race to God; nor of the causality of the Resurrection, as clearly asserted by Saint Paul.[76]

In Guerric of Igny we meet the bait-and-hook story and the implication of the Devil's rights; things which Tradition has laid aside after Saint Anselm and Saint Thomas. But we find also — without any elaborative speculation, which could merely have ruined them — the several aspects and the richness of teaching drawn from Scripture and the early Fathers, which are of lasting value and are more fully appreciated in our own day.

Speculation in strict categories is undoubtedly necessary if heresy and aberration are to be avoided. Yet we do well to recognize that, in the long run, we may come nearer to the

---

75. DS 1529 (Trent), 3891 (Encyclical *Humani generis*).

76. I can claim that this is the fruit of my own reflection, but I have found it clarified and have been encouraged to give expression to it upon reading Karl Rahner's contribution to the article *Salvation*, in *Sacramentum Mundi* V, pp. 425 s.

heart of the mystery if we are content to use symbol or allegory. For Saint Paul Christ was the new Adam. If Mary cooperated in the redemptive Incarnation, it was but a step for the Fathers to see in her the new Eve. Guerric is an heir to this tradition, which goes back to Justin and Irenaeus. "Today is the birthday of that new Mother, who has destroyed the curse brought by the first mother, so that all those who through the fault of the first had been born under the yoke of eternal condemnation, might instead through her inherit a blessing."[77]

77. Ser. 51, 1st for Our Lady's Birthday: 1; II, 192.

CHAPTER TEN

# THE WOUNDS OF CHRIST

QUITE CLEARLY Guerric attributes our Redemption and Renewal not simply to the Word made Flesh, but to Christ suffering and dying. "Through the blood of his cross making atonement for sins, he achieved the greatest triumph over princedoms and powers. . . ."[1]

As usual, he becomes yet more eloquent when he has recourse to figure and symbol. The wounds which Christ suffered when he died for us are holes in the rock where we may take refuge; they are a door in the side of the ark for those who would be saved from the rising waters of the flood. "Blessed is he who, that I might be able to build a nest in the clefts of the rock, let his hands, feet and side, be pierced; who opened his whole self to me, that I might go 'into the place of his wonderful tent,' might be protected 'in its hidden recess'." Then later: "What is the wound in Christ's side but the door in the side of the ark for those who are to be saved from the flood? "[2]

Any study which pretends to be scientific must investigate the sources of this devotion to the wounds of Christ. It may be still more important to take account of an author's influence upon later centuries.

"Devotion" to the wounds of Christ. This must not be misunderstood. The word "devotion" suggests to us today that one's attention to God is canalized through something

1. Ser. 30, 2nd for Palm Sunday: 2; II, 60.
2. Ser. 32, 4th for Palm Sunday: 5; II, 77, 78.

129

very particular, is realized in some one aspect of his self-communication to us; or that he seems to speak to us through one saint, the writings of one person, something concrete and even material, e. g. a relic, statue, medal or scapular of particular design or colour. The limitations of human nature being what they are, men are likely to need this at any time. The danger of exaggeration and even of superstition is obvious. But "devotion" of this kind is not prominent in the best religious teachers or in Fathers of the Church. It may be quite misleading to say of Guerric or any other of our Cistercian Fathers that they had "devotion" even to the humanity of Christ or to our Blessed Lady. With them in fact no one aspect of God's goodness or self-revelation is separated from the rest, but finds its place in the entire scheme. Their treatment is synthetic rather than analytic; they enjoy the panorama rather than fix their gaze upon one object with the aid of a telescope.

With this precaution we can investigate devotion to the sacred wounds in Guerric and in other Fathers of the Church.[3]

Saint Bernard speaks of those holes in the rock several times, and they are specially bound up with his commentary on the verse of the Song of Songs: "My dove in the clefts of the rock, in the hollows of the wall."[4] Both Bernard and Guerric would have received this interpretation under the name of Saint Gregory the Great, but in fact the text came from Robert of Tombelaine less than a century before: "By the clefts of the rock I would readily understand the wounds which Christ suffered in his hands and feet as he hung upon the cross. Just so the hollow in the wall would be for me the wound made by the lance as it pierced his side. It is fitting indeed that the dove is said to be in the clefts of the rock and the hollows of the wall. She remembers the cross and imitates Christ's long-suffering, calling to mind his wounds for her example. So it is that, like a dove in those clefts, the undi-

3. I am considerably indebted to Irenée Henriot, who wrote an *exercitatio* for licentiate at the Gregorian in 1955-6: *Les cisterciens et la dévotion aux plaies du Christ.* As far as I know, this has remained in typescript. See also DTC 4 (1): *Dévotion.*

4. Song 2:14.

vided soul finds in his wounds the food which strengthens her."[5]

Although this passage is not earlier than the eleventh century, the interpretation seems to have been given as far back as the sixth by Saint Justus, Bishop of Urgel: "My dove in the clefts of the rock . . . ; she dwells in the clefts of the rock, for she always finds hospitality in those wounds of Christ which have healed her."[6]

As for Saint Bernard, his passage shows a closer affinity to one in the Venerable Bede, and it is worth reading the texts side by side.[7] This is not irrelevant in a study of Guerric, for it will be clear how he is indebted to Bernard, probably directly to Bede as well, and to still another source.

BEDE: If, as the Apostle tells us, THE ROCK WAS CHRIST, what can the clefts in the rock be but the wounds which Christ endured for our salvation? In those clefts the dove dwells and builds her nest. So it is when any tender soul, or even the Church at large, puts her one hope of salvation in the Lord's Passion. She trusts that in the sacrament of his death SHE IS AS IT WERE PROTECTED FROM THE HAWK WHICH WOULD SNATCH HER. Whether her spiritual offspring be children or virtues, there she busies herself with bringing them to life.[8]

BERNARD: There is another [Bede? ] who expounds the place in this wise, understanding the clefts of the rock to be Christ's wounds. He is right indeed: FOR THE ROCK WAS CHRIST. Good are those clefts, where faith in his resurrection and godhead is built up. "My Lord and my God," we hear the Apostle saying. Where did he learn it, save in the clefts of the rock? Here the swallow has found her a home, and the turtle-dove a nest to lay her young. Here the dove IS PROTECTED, GAZING FEARLESSLY AT THE HAWK WHICH FLIES ALL AROUND HER. That is why he says: "My dove in the clefts of the rock."[9]

5. Robert, *On the Song of Songs* 2:15; PL 79:499D.
6. Justus of Urgel, *On the Song of Songs*; PL 67:972.
7. Cf. Eric Colledge, *The Mediaeval Mystics of England* (New York: Scribner, 1961), pp. 11, 12.
8. Bede, *On the Song of Songs* 2:9; PL 99:1111.
9. Bernard, *On the Song of Songs* 61:3; OB 2:149; CF 31.

Bernard's two obvious points of contact with Bede are the
assertion, "the rock was Christ," and the simile of the hawk. A
little later Bernard uses another text in the same way (Ps.
103:18), and for this his source would seem to be neither
Robert nor Bede, but Cassian.

| CASSIAN: Let him be covered by the enduring SHELTER OF THAT ROCK known to us from the gospel — spiritually A BADGER HIDING IN THE ROCK — that is in the memory of the Lord's Passion.[10] | BERNARD: THE ROCK IS A REFUGE FOR THE BADGERS. In truth, where can the weak find safety, secure lodging and rest, but in the Saviour's wounds.[11] |
|---|---|

Now at last we come to Guerric, who in one place combines both these two texts:

Blessed is he who, that I might be able to build a nest IN
THE CLEFTS OF THE ROCK, let his hands, feet and side,
be pierced. Blessed he who has opened his entire self to me,
that I may enter "the place of his wonderful tent" and be
protected in its hiding-place. THE ROCK IS INDEED A
REFUGE WELL SUITED TO THE BADGERS; no less is it
a welcome DWELLING PLACE FOR THE DOVES. These
clefts, so many open wounds all over his body, give pardon
to the guilty, grace to the righteous. Indeed he has a safe
dwelling place, my brethren, a tower of strength in the face
of the enemy, who lingers in the wounds of Christ by
devout and constant meditation. By faith and love of the
Crucified a man protects his soul from the heat of the flesh,
from the world's turmoil, FROM THE DEVIL'S AT-
TACK.[12]

The combination of the two texts suggest that Guerric depends upon Bernard, and so indirectly upon Bede and
Cassian. The devil is named openly, no longer under the simile of the hawk. However, some direct influence of Bede is

10. Cassian, Conf 10, ch. 11; SCh 54:91.
11. Bernard, *ibid.*
12. Ser. 32, 4th for Palm Sunday: 5; II, 77.

indicated by what Guerric says soon afterwards. The parallel texts are as follows:

BEDE: YOU SHALL MAKE A DOOR BELOW IN THE SIDE OF THE ARK .. It is fittingly commanded that the door should be placed in the side of the ark. It means the door opened by the soldier's lance IN THE SIDE OF OUR LORD AND SAVIOUR AS HE HUNG UPON THE CROSS. Straightway blood and water came out from it. It is through these sacraments that each of the faithful is received into the Communion of Holy Church as into the inner rooms of the ark.[13]

GUERRIC: WHAT IS THE WOUND IN CHRIST'S SIDE BUT THE DOOR IN THE SIDE OF THE ARK for those who are to be saved from the flood? But the one was a figure, the other is very truth, in which not only is mortal life preserved, but immortal life recovered. For in his loving kindness and compassion he opened his side, in order that the blood of the wound might give you life, the warmth of his body revive you, the breath of his heart flow into you as if through a free and open passage.[14]

So an influence of Bede upon Guerric is suggested by a combination of texts and interpretations in a single passage. It is still possible that Guerric could have taken the interpretation of the door in the ark straight from the same place as Bede. This is Saint Augustine's commentary on Saint John's 19th chapter, where Bede learned that the sacraments of the Church came from the side of Christ:

> "One of the soldiers opened his side with a lance." . . . that in a sense the door to life might there be opened, the door whence issued the Church's sacraments, without which no man can enter into that life which alone is worthy of the name. . . . . This was foretold by the door which Noah was commanded to make in the side of the ark. There those

13. Bede, *On Genesis* 6; CCL 118A: 108.
14. Ser. 32, 4th for Palm Sunday: 5; II, 78.

animals were to enter which should not perish in the flood; a figure of the Church.[15]

Consequently, the genealogy of devotion to the wounds of Christ may be something like that shown in the following diagram:

CLEFTS OF THE ROCK     THE DOOR IN THE ARK     THE ROCK A REFUGE
(*Song of Songs* 2:14)        (*Genesis* 6:16)       FOR THE BADGERS
                                                      (*Psalm* 103:18)

Justus of Urgel          Augustine          Cassian

             Bede

Pseudo-Gregory
(Robert of
Tombelaine)

                             Bernard

       Aelred
William of Saint Thierry     Guerric
      Amedeus
      à Kempis

If a line is drawn, e. g., through Augustine-Bernard-Guerric, this does not of course exclude the possibility or the likelihood, that Guerric drew immediately upon Augustine. The reason why a possible relationship is indicated (with dotted line) between Guerric and à Kempis is that manuscripts of Guerric were copied in à Kempis, part of the world. Indeed we shall soon be considering the possibility of Guerric's influence upon Jan Ruysbroeck.

Obviously these are only the sources and relationships which have been discovered in a limited research. No doubt there are others which may upset the genealogy. This is nothing more than provisional.

15. Augustine, *On John's Gospel*, 120:2; CCL 36:661; tr. H. Browne, 2 vols (Oxford, 1848-1849) 2:1046-1047.

The "clefts of the rock" theme became more common at this time among Cistercians and others besides. Here are the words of Saint Aelred of Rievaulx: " . . . let [the soul] linger in the clefts of the rock, in the hollows of the wall. For this while let her embrace you crucified, drink a draught of your sweetest blood."[16] Let William of Saint Thierry speak also: "Like Thomas, that man of desire, I would see and touch him all over. Not only that: I would draw near to the sacred wound in his side, the door made in the side of the ark. It would be enough for me to put my finger into it or all my hand. All my being would enter into the very heart of Jesus."[17]

Guerric is in the early stages of a devotion to the Passion and to the Wounds of Christ, which is to prevail all over the Western Church for centuries, and is at the beginning of our cult of the Sacred Heart. We hear of this later in such words as these of *The Imitation of Christ*: "Ah, but it is above your reach (you complain), such high contemplation of heavenly things. Why then, let your mind come to rest in Christ's Passion, and find in his sacred wounds the home it longs for. Take refuge in those wounds, those precious scars, as a devout soul should, and you will feel, in all your troubles, a deep sense of consolation. How little you will care for the contempt of your fellow men, how easily you will put up with their criticisms."[18]

This "devotion" is not so well received now. Was there too much appeal to sense? But how else can one speak to the ordinary man? Or there may have been such emphasis on the crucified and suffering Christ that men lost sight of the Incarnation Mystery as a whole, of the meaning of the Word Incar-

---

16. Aelred, *The Mirror of Charity* 1, 5, 16; CCL Cont Med 1:19; CF 17; *A Rule of Life for a Recluse* n. 31; CCL Cont Med 1:671; CF 2:90. Cf. Sermon 11 (1st for Easter), PL 195:276-277;CF 23.

17. William of Saint-Thierry, *On Contemplating God*, n. 3; CF 3:38. Cf. Amedeus of Lausanne, Homily 5; SCh 72:144; CF 18. If the diagram suggests an influence of Bernard upon William, the reverse is no less probable.

18. Thomas a Kempis, *The Imitation of Christ*, 2, 1, 4; tr. by Ronald Knox and Michael Oakley (1959), p. 61.

nate, suffering, risen, now reigning in glory, as the cause of
our sanctification. However that may be we should always
beware of going from one extreme to another, of forgetting
either that Christ did redeem us by his suffering and death; or
that our own following of Christ is meaningless without the
Cross. If we look outside the Roman Catholic Church we find
Dietrich Bonhoeffer insisting that the marvel of the Christian
revelation and the solution of our problems is a God who
suffers. The new Missal of Paul VI has continued to print for
thanksgiving after Mass a prayer which goes back to the four-
teenth century: "Soul of Christ, sanctify me. . . . O good
Jesu, hear me. Within thy wounds hide me."[19]

This much may be said for Guerric and for his companions,
that they would never have conceived of a spirituality which
had not the Word made Flesh at its center, or of a mystical
union which lost consciousness of Christ both God and Man.

19. See J. Bonnetti *Le stimate della Passione. Dottrina e Storia della devozione
alle cinque piaghe.* For *Anima Christi* see *Dictionnaire de Spiritualité* I, 670 (H.
Thurston).

# CHAPTER ELEVEN

# UNION WITH GOD THROUGH CHRIST

## THE NAKED TRUTH

THIS TRUTH IS CHRIST, both God and Man. Mary brings him to Simeon in the Temple, the Truth, but clothed in our human flesh. We know the truth from those who teach us, but it is not always easy to discern, for necessarily it is expressed in human language. The Mother Mary brings him clothed in flesh; Mother Church clothed in the word of the preacher. There is a third Mother, Grace, and she can bring the Truth unclothed, naked.

It is most necessary that this Truth should come to us clothed in flesh; clothed, too, in the words of those whom Christ has deputed to speak with authority. Guerric invites us, then, to come and receive the Truth in both these forms: " . . . he must come into the temple with Simeon and receive in his hands the Child whom his mother Mary brings; that is, embrace with devotion the Word of God, offered by Mother Church."[1] But we can expect more than this: "Not only is the Church a Mother to those who hear, but much more is Grace a Mother to those who pray. When you pray, this Mother Grace will give you the Child to embrace, provided that you come to the temple often and with devotion."

Now our author insists with emphasis and eloquence upon the unclothed nakedness of this Truth which is offered to us:

For him whom the Church offers to our ears by preaching, GRACE BRINGS INTO OUR HEARTS BY ENLIGHTEN-

---

1. Ser. 17, 3rd for Purification: 2; I, 115.

ING, MAKING HIM THE MORE PRESENT AND DE-
LIGHTFUL BY GIVING NAKED TRUTH TO SENSE
THAT IS PURE. The Truth which is Christ Mary gives us to
embrace clothed with flesh; the Church clothed in speech;
GRACE NAKED BY THE INPOURING OF THE SPI-
RIT. . . . For even though we cannot easily see the very
face of the highest Truth, and he is to be held great to
whom it is given to look upon that Truth "in a mirror
darkly," yet WHEN THE SPIRIT IS POURED INTO US,
WE FEEL SOMETHING OF HIM, AS IT WERE NAKED,
AND THAT SENSE OF OURS IS WARMED TO LOVE,
AS IT WERE BY FEELING HIS NAKED SELF.[2]

Guerric does not explain further what he means by the nakedness of this Truth; but perhaps there is no need. Our
ordinary experience of the Truth, which is Christ, comes
through some medium in which he is conveyed; here is an
experience which is direct and immediate.

### PASSING ON TO JAN RUYSBROECK

If it has been useful to trace Guerric's antecedents and
sources, it may be of still greater importance to show, if
possible, how he has influenced those who have come after
him. Since this can be no more than a beginning, we may be
allowed to pass over approximately two centuries, and to put
Guerric beside Jan Ruysbroeck, the Austin canon of Groe-
nendael.

This clearly needs some apology and explanation; which
may be presented in a series of propositions:

1) This theme of nakedness has been sought out in authors
who are likely to have been sources for Ruysbroeck: e. g.,
Saint Bernard, Saint Bonaventure, Richard of Saint Victor,
above all such works of Meister Eckhart as have been accessible. The idea is not in Saint Bernard's Purification sermons.[3]
Eckhart has a sermon on Simeon coming into the temple, but

2. *Ibid.*
3. Bernard, Sermons for Purification 1-3; OB 4:334-344; CF 10.

there is nothing like what we have read in Guerric.[4] If the "nakedness" theme has not been found, obviously this does not mean that it is not there. When someone else finds it, it will be possible to fill out the sketch here provided.

2) It seems true that Guerric was not much copied in manuscript, for we have found only nine codices from the two centuries following his death. However, his own town, Tournai, is on the border of the Low Countries, and Igny is not very far away. Four of the manuscripts used in our edition are from that part of Europe.

3) Guerric had some reputation after his death and the transcription of his sermons; enough for the sermons to be revised in the scriptorium of Clairvaux; also enough for a work to be published in his name, probably spuriously.[5]

4) If the idea that Ruysbroeck borrowed from Guerric should be inadmissible or refuted, then the influence may still be indirect. Above all we find Guerric at the beginning, or in the early stages, of a theme which has its final development among the Dutch and the English of the fourteenth-fifteenth centuries.

Certainly this idea of nakedness, of the naked truth, is very prominent and more fully explained in Ruysbroeck's writings. Furthermore, there is not the least doubt that Ruysbroeck was translated and read in England.[6] If Guerric influenced Ruysbroeck, even indirectly; then, indirectly also, he influenced our English spiritual tradition.

The connection suggested is all the more provisional, since it would more properly be demonstrated by one who was an expert on the Dutch mystics. I have been much captivated by Ruysbroeck, but chiefly by the *Adornment for Spiritual Marriage (De Gheestlijke Brulocht)* and for the most part by *The Perfection of the Sons of God*, also known as *The Sparkling Stone (Van den blinckenden Steen)*. Since this Sparkl-

---

4. Tr. of the works of Meister Eckhart by Franz Pfeifer (London, 1947), p. 64f.
5. "Liber amoris: was it written by Guerric of Igny? " Text presented and edited by J. Morson and H. Costello in *Cîteaux* 16 (1965) 114ff.
6. I have demonstrated this in a study which remains as yet in manuscript.

ing Stone is Jesus Christ himself,[7] it is evident that he is at the center of our contemplative life.

As for the idea of nakedness, or immediate union, recorded in Guerric — for Ruysbroeck it is usually man's own spirit that is called naked. But in one place we meet a nakedness which is God himself: "But while he is in possession of God, he will cling to A CERTAIN NAKEDNESS, BEREFT OF IMAGES, AND THAT IS GOD HIMSELF . . . He will be able to penetrate ever further and reach the inmost recesses of his Spirit, NAKED AND FREE OF EVERY IMAGE."[8] "By love we shall stay uplifted into THE UNCLOTHED NAKEDNESS OF OUR UNDERSTANDING."[9] "If we should abide with the Lord Jesus on Tabor, that is the mountain of OUR NAKED UNDERSTANDING."[10]

### IN ENGLAND: "THE CLOUD OF UNKNOWING"

There is no doubt that the Middle English work, *The Cloud of Unknowing,* is much indebted to Ruysbroeck. To prove this thoroughly would mean adding a chapter to a book on Guerric, and this would be somewhat out of proportion. For the moment it may be noted that works of Ruysbroeck are found in English manuscripts of the period, both in Latin and in English,[11] and it will be possible to indicate a direct borrowing. For the theme of nakedness, it may be useful to quote a few sentences from *The Cloud of Unknowing.*

" . . . thou findest but a darkness, and as it were a cloud of unknowing, thou knowest not what, saving that thou feelest in thy will a naked intent unto God.[12] . . . it is far better to

---

7. Rev 4:17.

8. Jan Ruysbroeck, *Calculus (The Sparkling Stone),* ch. 3, p. 513. References are to the Latin version, rendered by Surius the Carthusian, Köln, 1609.

9. *Ibid.* ch. 9, p. 523.

10. *Ibid.* ch. 12, p. 530.

11. Evidence of this has been collected by Eric Colledge: *The Treatise of Perfection of the Sons of God,* in *English Studies* 33 (Amsterdam, 1957), pp. 49-66.

12. References are to the version of *The Cloud of Unknowing,* with modernized vocabulary and spelling, edited by Justin McCann (edition of 1947). Ch. 3, p. 6. Those who are interested in the Middle English, in which the work was written, should see the critical edition by Phyllis Hodgson (London, 1944).

think upon the naked being of him and to love and praise him for himself.[13] . . . for naked intent directed unto God, without any other cause than himself, sufficeth wholly.[14] . . . For, as it is said before, the substance of this work is nought else but a naked intent directed unto God for himself. A naked intent, I call it. Because in this work a perfect prentice asketh neither releasing of pain, nor increasing of reward, nor (shortly to say) nought but himself."[15]

Here then is the theme of nakedness, noticed first in Guerric, developed further by Ruysbroeck, and under his influence in *The Cloud of Unknowing*. Ruysbroeck could indeed have taken it from a treatise *De adhaerendo Deo,* attributed to Saint Albert the Great;[16] but this is almost contemporary with Ruysbroeck himself.

### A MANUSCRIPT ANTHOLOGY OF RUYSBROECK

Miss Phyllis Hodgson, when she produced her valuable critical edition of *The Cloud,* made no mention of a manuscript which was one of its immediate sources. I owe my acquaintance with this manuscript to Eric Colledge (British Museum, Add. 37790). He calls it a translation of the *Calculus,*[17] but this account does not seem quite exact. Since at first reading it cannot be identified with any part of the *Calculus,* it may be thought a very free paraphrase, but in fact it is an anthology, Rusbrochian all the way through. In one place, it corresponds verbally with *The Cloud.* If the two passages are placed side by side, this will serve a double purpose. First it should establish the dependence of *The Cloud* upon the anthology; not vice versa, because of other external evidence; though it may be possible to find a common source from which both have drawn. In the second place it should help to explain the "nakedness" theme found first in Guer-

13. Ch. 5, p. 11.
14. Ch. 7, p. 13.
15. Ch. 24, p. 58.
16. *Beati Alberti Magni Opera omnia* (Paris, 1898) 37, 523-542. Translated into English by Elisabeth Stopp: *Of Cleaving to God* (London, 1954).
17. Eric Colledge, *art. cit.* p. 49.

ric: our union with God is to be immediate, without means or medium. Surius' Latin version of Ruysbroeck gives us repeatedly *sine modo,* or sometimes *modonescius*; another by Willem Jordaens usually *sine modo.* [18]

The words which correspond exactly are printed in capital letters. The texts are put in modern English:

| Anthology from *Calculus* (British Museum, add, ms. 37790. | *The Cloud,* ch. 34, p. 46. |
|---|---|
| No man may enter the said exercise by cleverness, for contemplative life may not be taught by another; but God, who is very Truth, manifests himself in spirit ... SUFFI-CIENTLY AND WITH-OUT MEANS MAY NO GOOD ANGEL STIR THY WILL; NOR, SHORTLY TO SAY, ANYTHING BUT ONLY GOD.... IN THIS WORK MEN SHALL USE NO MEANS, AND THAT MEN MAY NOT COME THERETO WITH MEANS. | And if it be thus, trust then steadfastly that it is only God that stirreth thy will and thy desire, plainly by himself, without means on his part or on thine ... for SUFFI-CIENTLY AND WITH-OUT MEANS MAY NO GOOD ANGEL STIR THY WILL; NOR, SHORTLY TO SAY, ANYTHING BUT ONLY GOD. So that thou mayest here by these words understand somewhat — but much more clearly by experience — that IN THIS WORK MEN SHALL USE NO MEANS, AND THAT MEN MAY NOT COME THERETO WITH MEANS. |

### BACK TO GUERRIC OF IGNY

All this has not been too far from Guerric. Whether Jan Ruysbroeck and his anthologist have drawn upon him or not,

18. Willem Jordaens: Latin version of *Calculus* in ms. Brussels, Bibl. Roy. 4935, edited with the Flemish original by D. Ph. Muller, Louvain, 1921.

they are in the same tradition, and they give us the further development of the theme which is so eloquently expressed in the third Purification sermon: "For him whom the Church offers to our ears by preaching, grace brings into our hearts by enlightening, making him the more present and delightful by giving naked truth to sense that is pure. . . . Grace gives us the Truth to embrace, Truth naked, by the inpouring of the Spirit. . . . When the Spirit is poured into us, we feel something of him, as it were naked, and that sense of ours is warmed to love, as it were by feeling his naked self."[19]

All along the nakedness theme has several nuances; indeed it may seem at first sight that it means several different things. It may refer to God's Being, as in *The Cloud*; in the same work to the "naked intent," asking "neither releasing of pain, nor increasing of reward," the absence of all thought and images, as in Ruysbroeck. Basically, however, the meaning is always the same: immediacy; nothing between the soul and God.

## MYSTICAL UNION

When a piece of writing is so elegantly prepared and polished as is usually found in Guerric of Igny or Bernard of Clairvaux, there is some distance which separates the writing from experience, from real life. Let us, however, define mystical prayer as direct experience of the presence of God. We may then find some passages, and be sure that they are not mere rhetoric; without real experience they could never have been written. If there is anything in Guerric (we may almost say in the twelfth century) which gives expression to such meeting with God, it is the place transcribed above.

If the words describe such an experience, we have all the more right to put the same interpretation upon other places as well. Thus in an earlier sermon we hear that Simeon was consumed by a love which tormented at the same time as it gave delight: "Truly, in the quiet contentment of old age you

19. Ser. 17, 3rd for Purification: 2; I, 115.

carried this light not simply in your hands, but in the very
dispositions of your heart. . . . O tinder of love, so sweet a
love and tender to re-enkindle the heart, sweet and tender
still when it grieves and tortures; a delightful torture of happiness, like the burning glow of health refreshed.."[20]

THE TIME OF DESIRE

This remains the time of desire, however close our union
with God. Simeon is the figure of those whose desires are on
the point of fulfillment. Nothing is left but for him to sleep
in peace. Or rather it is not a sleep; it is having his youth
renewed like that of an eagle, standing in God's presence and
enjoying a vision which is eternal peace:

> Such was Simeon, that old man of ours, as much to be
> desired as he was full of desires. Long before this, I think,
> the days of his purification had been completed. Today the
> days of his expectation are completed also. Now therefore,
> as the Lord has said, nothing remains for him, after seeing
> the Lord's Christ, peace of God and man, but to be sent
> away in peace, and in that same peace to sleep. This means
> to be taken to Jerusalem, the vision of eternal peace, and to
> be present before the Lord, to contemplate the peace
> which surpasses all our understanding. O Simeon, man of
> desires, your desire of good things is fulfilled. O blessed old
> man, your youth is renewed like the eagle's.[21]

Even if, with Christ, the fullness of time has come to us, it is
a fullness which is overflowing with desire; *desiderantissima
plenitudo temporis.* [22] In this time of waiting all that is asked
of us is that we should never turn our eyes away from the
Son of God who has come to us as a Child:

20. Ser. 15, 1st for Purification: 2; I, 101.

21. Ser. 19, 5th for Purification: 1; I, 127. I have discussed elsewhere the sense
in which we continue to desire both here and in our final beatitude (*epektasis*): J.
Morson, "Seeking God by Desire," *Cistercian Studies* 2 (1967), 175-185.

22. When I first met this word, I thought that there was a copyist's error, since
the printed editions had always given *desideratissima.* In fact the manuscripts are
unanimous in supporting *desiderantissima,* and I have found the word elsewhere.
See SCh 166:221, note 2.

We can be certain, brethren, that if we do not turn away our face from the contemplation of him who lies in the manger, we can feed most happily on the very look of him, and we shall say: "The Lord feeds me and I lack nothing; he has settled me in a place of pasture." Then indeed we shall know that the fullness of time yearning with desire has come, in which God has sent his Son, through whom we are already satisfied with such a fullness of good things. To him be blessing and thanksgiving now and through endless ages. Amen.[23]

Our chapter on Redemption has then brought us to a mystical union which is its choicest fruit. It has brought us back, too, to the Child in the manger with whom we began our meditations upon Christ in Gurric of Igny.

23. Ser. 9, 4th for Christmas: 5; I, 60.

# CONCLUSION

HESE FEW REFLECTIONS have shown us something of Guerric the abbot, preacher, and spiritual guide. The theologian—he is certainly this in the oldest and most genuine sense, since he can speak to us of God from the abundance of his own intimacy and experience. To what extent would he be recognized as a theologian today? He is not what we mean by a scholastic; he may not have read Saint Anselm; the subtleties of an Abelard or of a Gilbert Porreta pass him by. Anything that he knows of these men he has learned from their opponents: from William of Saint Thierry, from Saint Bernard, from the condemnations of Councils. The most that he will do in speculation about the Persons of the Trinity runs to a few lines in his Rogation sermon, and he undertakes this with hesitation, fear and trembling. "Who is able to understand? Who can explain? Or who can meditate worthily on the ineffable mystery of the Blessed Trinity? How the Father is of himself alone, the Son is from the Father and the Holy Spirit is from both Father and Son, and how there are three Persons in a unity of substance." In our own day he would almost be called an obscurantist, for he goes on to say that to speculate on this mystery or to discuss it belongs to heretics: "That foolish woman, the audacious vanity of heretics, incites itching ears to unravel such mysteries. But we must believe in God, not take him to pieces." The only thing within his reach is not the Trinity of Persons, but rather the trinity of ideas which he can have of them.

Those divine Persons are not the three leaves which he can break to those who come to his table: "So let us leave those loaves, which may be broken only by such as have the lofty stature of angels, until we have grown and are on an equality with them, worthy to eat at their table."[1]

It is true enough that the future abbot of Igny was almost certainly educated in the cathedral school of Tournai, that he can hardly have escaped some intellectual influence of Odo of Cambrai, that he should have made some contact with the scholastic movement which began with Saint Anselm. The biographer of Hugh of Marchienne tells us that Guerric was *magister apud Tornacum*. In whatever sense this is strictly accurate, it must have some historical foundation.[2]

However, the only real evidence for a man's attainments as a theologian is to be found in the writings which he has left to us. That Guerric was a theologian — this cannot be disputed, unless the word is given a very narrow, even an arbitrary sense.[3] But any special influence of the eleventh-twelfth century cathedral school is not easily detected. He would seem to be indebted to that early formation chiefly in his capacity to elucidate ideas and to give expression to them.

When Guerric, no longer a young man, became abbot of Igny, he had been away from Tournai for thirteen years or more. That was time enough for him to forget definitions, distinctions, arguments, which were no longer likely to serve a purpose; time enough, too, for a man once formed intellectually to acquire knowledge richer and more profound than could be had from the controversies of the schools.

The influences which can be discerned in the sermons — at least by the writer of these pages — are not those of Tournai. But it has been impossible not to recognize the accents of William of Saint Thierry and of Saint Bernard. Through them and through Guerric are transmitted the voices of Leo,

1. Ser. 36, Rogation Days: 3-4; II, 101.
2. CF 8, Introduction, pp. ix-xii.
3. A general and summary account of Guerric's theology has been given in the Introduction to CF 8, pp. xxviii-xxxviii, followed by a fuller development of a selected theme.

Augustine, Ambrose, Gregory and Bede; sometimes even of Origen, Evagrius and Cassian.[4] It was to them that the monk listened in the choir stall; their pages that he may have been able to turn in the reading-cloister of Clairvaux. That was no idle exercise if it was undertaken by a genius already well formed.

If the teaching of Fathers such as these was being passed on, it follows that the Bible was being quoted and interpreted on every page. A cursory reading of Guerric's text shows that this was being done. He is well aware that Tradition has recognized three senses of Scripture, but he dwells chiefly upon the allegorical; all things lead to Christ. The brethren have a right to some conclusion which bears upon their lives and conduct; but this does not involve an artificial passing from an allegorical to a moral sense. Even to distinguish the two is hardly necessary, for if Scripture has received an allegorical interpretation, the moral is there already. The Mystery which has redeemed us is already a norm for our way of life.[5]

But if Guerric has declined the speculation of the schools, there is still another way of knowing, indeed of going deeper into what God has revealed. It is not for us in this life to look upon the face of Divine Truth. Our knowledge of all things comes by means of the shadows which they cast over us. As for God, we do not even perceive his shadow, unless it should happen that the Eternal Day breathe on us. What we then see is glorious and lightsome, but it remains a shadow of what really is.[6] Therefore we give a more true expression to this reality by the symbols and types which the Spirit of God, speaking through the inspired books, has destined for this purpose, than by using any of the concepts or categories of ordinary human knowledge.

Here, then, are Guerric's chief preoccupations. Unlike

---

4. To indicate these sources was the main purpose of the notes accompanying the critical text in SCh 166.

5. Ser. 27, 2nd for Annunciation: 4; II, 44. Ser. 18, 4th for Purification: 1; I, 120.

6. Ser. 46, 3rd for SS. Peter and Paul: 3-4; II, 162-164.

Bernard, or even Aelred, he is not concerned with polemics, episcopal appointments, the morals of the higher clergy, the reform of the Curia. If Bernard has to interrupt his sermons on the Song of Songs to deal with a schism in the Church, must devote two of those sermons to the refutation of a nascent heresy,[7] all that we expect or receive from Guerric is a tranquil conduct through the Church's year, meditating without distraction upon the mysteries of our renewal and redemption.

The literary style of a Bernard or of a Guerric befits the task assigned by Providence to each. Bernard knows how to denounce in tones that could never come from Guerric's calmer temperament. Bernard rises also to lyrical heights, which by themselves could suffice to secure him an immortal memory. Guerric writes always with elegance; as a general rule perhaps more on the level of the simple reader, and easier to recommend to those who are living eight centuries later. Often his sermons have a beauty, which does not compel the attention so immediately as one of Bernard's choicest passages, but rests in the memory and suffices to bring the reader back to him. Bernard is sometimes the thunder and lightning, sometimes the blaze of noon, in the more sultry Burgundy. Guerric is rather the evening sun in a pale blue sky, lighting up the waters of the northern seas.[8]

Christ, God made Man, is at the center of all that Guerric has had to tell us. He is the Stone hewn without hands of men from the Rock which is the Virgin Mary; at the same time he is every word coming from the mouth of God, himself the Bread on which he feeds, the Bread which we share with him at the supper to which we are invited. If we have looked for spiritual nourishment, we have found no need to go elsewhere than to this teaching concerning Christ.

His becoming a Child in the Virgin's womb is his utmost humiliation; but at the same time it is his triumph. He reigns

7. Bernard, *On the Song of Songs*: between sermons 24 and 25; sermons 65, 66.

8. I have already raised the hypothesis of some influence of Guerric upon the Flemish, and so indirectly the English: pp. 138-42.

there from the ivory throne, accomplishing the work for which his Father has sent him into the world. As the Eternal Word he comes from the Father by way of knowledge, contemplating in eternity. His advent in this time of waiting, our being transformed into his image, are simply a participation of this; we can contemplate his eternal glory, even as though through a mirror.[9] It is for this that we are invited to his side. Mary is there, too, as a model; so that with her we may turn all these things over in our heart.[10]

Already we are renewed. Redemption and renewal have several aspects for Guerric. Outstanding among them is the oneness of Christ with our humanity. He has suffered, died and risen: here is the "example" — more than this: the "proof," "cause," "sacrament"[11] of what is to be brought about in us. Of first and last importance is this: the Son of God stands as one of us before the Father. "Already my being is with you."[12]

Has this study justified its title: *Christ the Way*? He tells us that he is "the Way, the Truth and the Life."[13] Christ is indeed the Truth which we are to contemplate now, our Blessed Life for all eternity. If we would go to the Father, there is no other Way. "Lead me in the eternal way; that through you, the Way and the Truth, I may come to you, the Truth and Life eternal. Glory to you for eternal ages. Amen."[14]

---

9. Ser. 2, 2nd for Advent: 4; I, 12.
10. Ser. 28, 3rd for Annunciation: 6; II, 53-54.
11. Ser. 34, 2nd for Easter: 1; II, 86.
12. Ser. 1, 1st for Advent: 1; I, 1.
13. Jn 14:6.
14. Ser. 4, 4th for Advent: 5; I, 29.

# ABBREVIATIONS

Note: References to Guerric himself and to other Cistercian Fathers are made, when possible, to the CISTERCIAN FATHERS SERIES. The two volumes of Guerric's Sermons have been published in volumes 8 and 32. Any reference gives the number of the Sermon as found in this edition, the title of the Sermon and the paragraph number, and then the volume and page number. E.g., Ser. 35, 3rd for Easter: 4; 11, 95.

| | |
|---|---|
| ACW | Ancient Christian Writers (Westminster, Md., Paramus, N.J.: Newman, 1947–). |
| CCL | Corpus christianorum, series Latina (Turnhout: Brepols, 1945–). |
| CF | Cistercian Fathers Series (Spencer, Mass., Washington, D.C.: Cistercian Publications, 1970–). |
| Coll | *Collectanea O.C.R.* later *Collectanea Cisterciensia.* |
| Cont med | Continuatio mediaevalis of CC. |
| Conf. | Jean Cassien. *Conférences.* SCh 42, 54, 65 (1955, 1958, 1959). Tr. G. Scannell, Cistercian Studies Series 20, 31. |
| Div | Bernard of Clairvaux. *Sermones de diversis;* OB 6-1. *Occasional Sermons;* CF 45-46. |
| DS | *Enchiridion Symbolorum.* Ed. H. Denzinger and A. Schönmetzer (New York: Herder, 1967). |
| Ep | Letter(s). |
| FC | Fathers of the Church (New York; Washington, D.C.: Catholic University, 1947–). |
| GCS | *Die griechischen christlichen Schriftstellen* (Leipzig-Berlin, 1897–). |
| LF | Library of the Fathers (Oxford: Parker, 1844-1877). |
| LSB | Bernard of Clairvaux. *Letters.* Tr. B. S. James, *The Letters of St. Bernard of Clairvaux* (London: Burns Oates, 1953). |

OB      *Sancti Bernardi Opera.* Ed. J. Leclercq, C. H. Talbot, H. M. Rochais (Rome: Editiones Cistercienses, 1957—).

PG      Patrologiae cursus completus, series Graeca. 161 vols. (Paris: Migne, 1856-1866).

PL      Patrologiae cursus completus, series Latina. 216 vols. (Paris: Migne, 1844-1864).

SC      Bernard of Clairvaux, *Sermones super Cantica Canticorum.* OB 1 and 2. Tr. K. Walsh, CF 4, 7, 31, 40.

SCh     Sources chrétiennes (Paris: Cerf, 1943—).

TCC     *The Teaching of the Catholic Church as Contained in Her Documents.* Ed. J. Neuner, H. Roos, K. Rahner (Cork: Gill, 1966).

# BIBLIOGRAPHY

## MANUSCRIPTS AND PRINTED EDITIONS AND TRANSLATIONS

*Sermons.* Introduction, critical text and notes by John Morson and Hilary Costello. French tr. made under the direction of Placide Deceille. 2 vols. SCh 166 (1970), 202 (1973). For mss and earlier eds. of Latin text, see "Introduction," ch. 3 pp. 69-80.

*Liturgical Sermons.* Tr. Monks of Mount Saint Bernard Abbey. 2 vols. CF 8, 32 (1970-1971). This is the first complete English tr. of the Sermons.

*The Christmas Sermons of Bl. Guerric of Igny.* Tr. Sister Rose of Lima. Introductory essay by Thomas Merton. Abbey of Gethsemani, 1959.

*Two Sermons for the feast of St. Benedict.* Ed., tr., and annotated by monks of Mount Saint Bernard Abbey. *Monastic Studies* 3 (1965) 1-17.

## BIOGRAPHICAL SOURCES

St Bernard. Letter 89, to Oger, a canon regular, n. 3. Letter 90, to the same, n. 2. PL 182:221B-222B. In *The Letters of Saint Bernard.* Tr. by Bruño Scott James. London: Burns Oates, 1953, letters 92, 93; pp. 137-139.

*Charters* of the diocese of Tournai, most not edited. Here the author has relied entirely upon guidance and information given by Dom Nicholas Huyghebaert OSB.

*Exordium Magnum Cisterciense* (Distinction 3, chapters 8-9). Ed. Bruno Griesser. Rome: *Editiones cistercienses,* 1961.

Herman, *Liber restaurationis abbatiae Sancti Martini Tornacensis*; PL 180:41f.

*Vita Hugonis, abbatis Marchianensis.* Ed. E. Martène and U. Durand. *Thesaurus novus anecdotorum III,* Paris, 1717, col. 1709-1736.

## STUDIES

Aleth (Sister), "L'abbaye du Bienheureux Guerric: Notre-Dame d'Igny," *Coll.* 19 (1957), 300-317.

Beller, J., *Le Bienheureux Guerric, disciple de Saint Bernard et second abbé de Notre-Dame d'Igny de l'Ordre de Cîteaux au diocèse de Reims*, Reims, 1890.

Bouyer, L., *The Cistercian Heritage*. Westminster, Md.: Newman, 1958. Ch. 8: *Guerric of Igny: the Heritage of Cîteaux*, pp. 190-204.

Costello, H., "The Meaning of Redemption in the Sermons of Guerric of Igny," *Cîteaux* 17 (1966), 281-303.

Decabooter, A., "L'optimisme de Guerric d'Igny," *Coll.* 19 (1957), 249-272.

Dereine, C., "Odon de Tournai et la crise du cénobitisme au XIe siécle,"*Revue du Moyen Age latin* 4 (1948), 137-154.

De Wilde, D., *De Beato Guerrico abbate Igniacensi eiusque doctrina de formatione. Christi in nobis*. Westmalle, 1935. Exerpt: "The Formation of Christ in Us: Bl. Guerric of Igny," *Monastic Studies* 2 (1964), 29-45.

D'Haenens, A., *Moines et clercs à Tournai au début du XIIe siècle: La vita commune del clero nei secoli XI e XII*. Atti della settimana di studio, Mendola, 1959, Milan, 1962.

Fracheboud, A., "Le charme personnel du Bienheureux Guerric," *Coll.* 19 (1957), 222-237.

Gatterer, M., "Der selige Guerricus und seine Sermones," *Zeitschrift für Katholische Theologie* 19 (1895), 35-90.

Gonzalez, J., "El beato Guerrico interprete de San Pablo," *Cistercium* 9 (1957), 243-250.

Leclercq, J., "Guerric et l'école monastique," *Coll.* 19 (1957), 238-248.

——, *Recueil d'études sur saint Bernard et ses écrits* I. Rome, 1962. Part I, ch. 8: *La collection des sermons de Guerric d'Igny*.

Louf, A., "Une théologie de la pauvreté monastique chez le Bienheureux Guerric d'Igny," *Coll.* 20 (1958), 207-222, 362-373.

Merton, T., *The Christmas Sermons of Blessed Guerric of Igny*. Gethsemani, U.S.A., 1959.

Milcamps, R. and Dubois, A., "Le Bienheureux Guerric. Sa Vie, son Oeuvre," *Coll.* 19 (1957), 207-221.

Miquel, P., "L'expérience de Dieu selon Guerric d'Igny," *Coll.* 32 (1970), 325-328.

Morson, J. and Costello, H., "Liber amoris: Was it written by Guerric of Igni?," *Cîteaux* 16 (1965), 114-135 (text edited and presented).

——, *Dictionnaire de Spiritualité* 6 (1967): article *Guerric d'Igny*, col. 1113-1121.

——, "Who was Guerric of Igny?" *Downside Review* 84 (1966), 57-75.

Péchenard, P. L., *Histoire de l'Abbaye d'Igny de l'Ordre de Cîteaux au diocèse de Reims*. Reims, 1883.

Pennington, M. B., "Guerric of Igny and his sermons for the Feast of the Assumption," *Studia monastica* 12 (1970), 87-96.

——, "Together unto God. Contemplative Community in the Sermons of Guerric of Igny," *Studia monastica* 14 (1972), 75-89.

Thomas, R., "Le Bienheureux Guerric et Notre Dame," *Coll.* 16 (1954), 287-295. *Ibid.* 17 (1955), 110-118.

*Note*: Several of these studies have been cited from *Coll.* 19 (1957). That year was the eighth centenary of Guerric's death, and an entire issue was devoted to him: fascicule 3, 201-330.

### OTHER WORKS CONSULTED

(Compilation) *Bernard de Clairvaux*, Historical Commission of the Order of Cîteaux, Paris, 1953.

(ed. Phillis Hodgson) *The Cloud of Unknowing*. Early English Text Society, n. 218, 1944: rpt. 1973.

(ed. Justin McCann) *The Cloud of Unknowing*, modernized version. Orchard Books, 1947, 1960.

Colledge, Eric, *The Mediaeval Mystics of England*. New York: Scribner, 1961.

——, *The Treatise of Perfection of the Sons of God. English Studies* 33 (Amsterdam, 1957), 49-66.

Galot, Jean, "Science et Conscience de Jésus," *Nouvelle Revue Théologique* 82 (1960), 113-121.

Galtier, Paul, *L'Unité du Christ: Être-Personne-Conscience,* 1939.

Leclercq, J., *The Love of Learning and the Desire for God*. New York: Fordham, 1961.

Lonergan, Bernard, *De constitutione Christi ontologica et psychologica*. Rome, 1958.

De Lubac, Henri, *Exégèse médiévale*. 2 vols. Paris: Aubier, 1959-1964.

Marmion, Columba, *Sponsa Verbi*. London: Sands, 1925.

Morson, John, "The English Cistercians and the Bestiary," *Bulletin of John Rylands Library* 39 (1956), 146-170.

——, "Seeking God by Desire," *Cistercian Studies* 2 (1967), 175-185.

Olier, Jean Jacques, *Catéchisme de la Vie Intèrieure,* in *Oeuvres complètes* . . . , (1856).

Rahner, Karl, *Current Problems in Christology. Theological Investigations* I. Baltimore: Helicon, 1961. pp. 149-200.

——, *Dogmatic Reflections on the Knowledge and Self-Consciousness of Christ. Theological Investigations* V. Baltimore: Helicon, 1966, pp. 193-215.

# CISTERCIAN PUBLICATIONS

*Titles Listing*

1978

## THE CISTERCIAN FATHERS SERIES

### THE WORKS OF BERNARD OF CLAIRVAUX

### THE WORKS OF WILLIAM OF ST THIERRY

### THE WORKS OF AELRED OF RIEVAULX

### THE WORKS OF GUERRIC OF IGNY

### OTHER CISTERCIAN WRITERS

## THE CISTERCIAN STUDIES SERIES

### EARLY MONASTIC TEXTS

### MONASTIC STUDIES

### CISTERCIAN STUDIES

### BY DOM JEAN LECLERCQ